When
Children
Ask

When Children Ask

MARGUERITTE HARMON BRO

Revised Edition

HARPER & ROW, PUBLISHERS

New York and Evanston

WHEN CHILDREN ASK, REVISED EDITION

Copyright, 1940, 1956, by Margueritte Harmon Bro
Printed in the United States of America

Library of Congress catalog card number: 55-6782

B-T

To My Parents
Andrew Davidson Harmon
Alice Gadd Harmon
who will question some of the answers
suggested in this book and answer some
of the questions they will read
between the lines

Foreword

In 1938 when an opportunity came my way to go to Argentina to visit an old uncle, I found myself quartered for two and a half months on a small Swedish freighter with only one other passenger, a disconcerting amount of quiet, and an absence of useful activity positively upsetting to the mother of four energetic children. Soon exhausting the ship's resources, I took to standing for hours at the prow and was finally reduced to thinking. Those were revealing thoughts and what they first revealed was an astounding number of occasions when I wished we had done differently in meeting our own children's needs, but also enough satisfactory occasions so that one might continue fresh-hearted in the task of being a parent. Then I considered our friends who were trying to meet like needs in their children. And finally I decided to write a book about the different ways in which parents deal with the same questions.

At that time our children were spread from second grade to first-year college. Now two of our sons, our daughter, and a near-daughter who lived with us for some years, are married. And there are thirteen grandchildren. The family is wiser by seventeen members and a kind of geometrical increase in mistakes and achievements. Also during the intervening years our lives have been bound in, one way and another, with the problems of other people's boys and girls. Ten years on a college campus brought to the fore the acute considerations of adolescents in regard to dating, premarital standards, marriage, and often the psychological uncertainties growing out of the divorce of parents.

At the same time the young were raising new questions rooted in the demands of new experience precipitated by the Second World War and the ensuing compulsory military training. Also questions derived from developments in mathematics and physics, including the atom bomb; the development of television; the expansion of air travel and the shrinkage of space; likewise questions about competing ideologies.

Rather recently, two years spent in Southeast Asia, some acquaintance with the problems of the young in Korea and Japan, observation in other parts of Asia and Europe, have pointed up a common denominator in the religious questions young people are asking everywhere. To attempt definitive answers would be presumptuous. Indeed, to deal with the questions at all one needs to have, with Confucious, no foregone conclusions; with Lao-tze, a capacity for understanding while remaining unnoticed; with Buddha, a passion to *be* before teaching; with Jesus, a sense of retaining the child's approach to life. The last is the hardest and perhaps includes the others, for a child comes freshly at a situation, gives his whole interest to the object of his attention without self-consciousness, and has a natural joyousness which one suspects is the climate of insight. These qualities of a good answerer my husband has to a far greater degree than I shall ever have, but by the time we are great-grandparents—when I expect to revise these pages once more—perhaps some of these qualifications may have brushed off on me.

It is surprising to note the changes in the religious climate since the first writing of this book. Currently interest in prayer is open, eager, unapologetic; extrasensory experience is acknowledged as relevant to religious interest and

perhaps scientifically important; concern for the ecumen-
icity of the church has softened denominational lines. Not
only children but parents are asking more insistent and
pertinent questions about the dimensions of life, the meaning of death, and the relevance of immortality.

The last sentence in the original foreword to this volume
should stand: Any parent will understand automatically
the hesitation and honest-to-goodness humility with which
any other parent tries to report what goes on in the mind
of a child.

Contents

When
Children
Ask

I. Parents Who Answer

And children's faces looking up
Holding wonder like a cup.

Success in rearing children seems to consist largely in accomplishing the impossible without effort. The wonder is that we live and grow at all in the face of the high demands of our offspring. But we do. We even have our little islands of serenity upon which we stand looking upstream and down, wondering at the reefs we have passed safely, measuring the current ahead. Sometimes, for our own sake or someone else's, we pause to draw a sort of outline map of our journeys — using a light pencil — knowing that the course probably looked different to the others who were with us, remembering that our own sense of direction went askew now and then. Just the same, if we cannot stamp our map "official" — if we cannot say, "This is *the* way to bring up children" — it is something to know a hazard when we've passed it, or when it looms in the offing.

Probably the most difficult hazard which parents have to negotiate is the fact that when a child asks a question, no matter how suddenly, the parent has to reply whether he knows the answer or not. If he wants to maintain an enduring relationship between himself and his child, one upon which the winds may beat and the rains may fall, then it is just plain necessary for him to come through with an answer. But only a paragon could be prepared beforehand with all the answers, and a paragon, he consoles himself, would no doubt give his child a dreadful inferiority complex. No ordinary parent can even guess in what direction a child's mind is going to move because his next question may not have any apparent relationship to the things he has previously been saying and doing.

But in this matter of answering when he does not know what to say a parent eventually makes a discovery, namely, that if he does not know the answer to his child's questions offhand, then he has to go find out the answer and come back to share it. Becoming a good answerer is as simple as that, and as relentless. The parent of a questioner becomes an answerer only by unceasing endeavor and unremitting honesty in finding out. Lazy minds beget lazy minds, and haziness and laziness have more in common than seven-eighths of their letters.

On the other hand, when parents are as eager as their children to find the answers to things, then the children are already half-answered. The spirit of joint inquiry is probably chief among the bridges of integrity which span the gap between generations.

Now any parent knows a large, important question when he hears it, but the odd thing is that little questions are just as important as big ones because it is the questioning which matters. Questions are the child's growing edge. He has no other way to grow. Questions are his hold upon his universe. He has no other way to take hold. Thwart a thousand little roots and the tree is never made fast in the earth. A child in the same fashion takes hold of life by the hair roots without which the main roots cannot be fed.

Tommy is dressing, or supposed to be, when his mother notes that actually he is only standing in a listening attitude, shoes and stockings in his hands. Before she can remonstrate, he asks, "Why does the radiator make that noise?"

"It's the steam," says his mother. "Tommy, I wish you'd get dressed."

"But what is the steam doing?" Tommy persists.

"How should I know?" says mother. "You'll be late for kindergarten if you don't get dressed."

This mother is no answerer.

Another sort of mother might take a minute to explain: "These radiators are heated by steam which comes up through pipes from the boiler down in the basement. Sometimes when the radiators cool off, a part of that steam condenses into water and then when the janitor makes up another hot fire and the steam comes up again, it has to bubble through the collected water until the water gets hot enough to be steam, too. So it's the steam bubbling through the water that makes the noise you hear."

This second mother is a "natural" answerer. (Of course, the noise Tommy heard may have been a different noise with a different explanation.) To be sure, the second mother may precipitate six dozen further questions about steam and have to explain every word she uttered in her original explanation. The breakfast hour may become an elementary physics class. But few breakfasts are put to as good use as that, and talk about steam may be at least as interesting as talk about who burned the toast. This second mother is a first-class answerer because, in this instance, she is armed with facts pertinent to the question at the moment of its asking.

But perhaps Tommy's mother really has not the least idea what makes the noise in the radiator. She has often wondered herself but never asked because she was sure she would not understand if someone told her. For herself she can accept the responsibility of not finding out. But she has no right to make such a choice for her child. His question, no matter how remote it may seem to her, is his right to an answer. Even if she wants to make a poet of her son, she has no right to withhold the answer to the radiator's racket, because her young poet may find his rhythm in steam and boilers, in pistons, cylinders and driving power. Or her son's creativity may not be the poet's creativity at all. It may be the physicist's creativity stirring him to question.

A third mother who does not know the facts involved says frankly: "I don't know what makes that noise. It's got something to do with steam. But we can find out from the janitor." (This is allowing for the chance that the child's father may not be steam-minded, either.) And then she finds out. She may even postpone her shopping trip or otherwise rearrange her morning to get that answer. It will not take long. Tommy cannot absorb a great deal of information but he needs as much answer as he can use.

This mother also becomes a first-rate answerer. Moreover, she will probably keep right on finding out as long as her son keeps on asking. In a sense hers may be a hard life in the way that an explorer's life or a scientist's life or a philosopher's life is hard because there will always be one more thing to find out. She can never take an examination and graduate. She has to live all the time in the seek-and-answer mood. Her reward is that she does indeed live and grow, even though a parent. Her child grows too.

Of course, the second and third mothers may be the same mother, for the most determined mother cannot know all the answers. But in either case she speaks with authority because there is no less authority in the honest quest than in the immediate factual answer.

One of the relentless aspects of a child's development

is the way in which he utilizes whatever material may be at hand to build his universe. If he cannot get facts, he builds anyway. The only difference is that he rears a dizzy structure which will later have to be torn down and rebuilt. Obviously a waste of time and energy, for it is so much easier for a child to add to and undergird the simple framework of his early construction than to have to knock out whole sections of wall and foundation. Build he must. The only problem is what sort of materials he will have to use. Fortunately honest materials for building a reliable universe can now be had in book form keyed to any age group and representing almost any field of inquiry. Less fortunately, parents may become parents without knowing a thing about such books or feeling any responsibility for making them available to the child through home, school, or public library. We have not yet reached the day when the state requires minimum knowledge tests of parents-to-be. It seems ridiculous that a small child's questions about the world around him should customarily be met with such parental vagueness. Respect for and co-operation with natural law depends so directly upon understanding that the marvel is we dare to be indifferent about our ignorance and unashamed in acknowledging it.

Of course, there comes a time when a child's quest for answers has to be passed on to the child himself. Indeed, one test of a question's validity is the child's willingness to exert himself to find an answer. A parent usually senses the difference between hazy wondering and a real desire to know; he senses when the child is using delaying tactics by musing aloud and when he really has his curiosity aroused; if he is alert he also senses when to stir a musing into genuine curiosity. If the child is old enough to understand the custodian's answer about the steam in the pipes, then he can jolly well go in quest of the knowledge himself and come back with his conquest to share with his mother — who had better listen and understand if she wants her own future explanations attended.

The matter of motivating a child to find his own answers can be tricky. Andy is in Junior High, failing in Community Studies for lack of bringing his notebook to date, when his father issues an ultimatum: no notebook, no play.

"Let me see those questions," says the father.

With a weary gesture the boy hands them over.

"Every answer is in this year's *World Almanac* and right here is the *Almanac*." His father takes it off the shelf, his tone sharpening to sarcasm as he asks, "Can you use an index?"

Andy's answer has a bored resignation, without impudence or presumption. "You look up the answers and I'll copy them into the book."

There is no resignation in his father's reply. "You get up off that chair..."

Book in hand, Andy starts for the door, stops in his tracks, looks at his dad and asks a real question. "Why should I? I don't want to know the answers. I don't care if I fail in Community Studies because if I ever want to know all that stuff when I'm grown up, I'll get my secretary to look it up. You just want me to do a lot of silly work because your pride's hurt when I fail. But my pride isn't hurt. Why should I hunt answers I don't want to know?"

Now that father has to think fast in order to give some validity to the step-by-step process of learning, to the possible advantages of mental exertion, the necessity for a public school system's being geared to averages, the social factors in classroom experience, the psychological justification for parental pride. Gradually the two of them settle into sweet reasonableness and the mood of the discussion becomes more important than any exchange of opinion.

Not infrequently the mood of a question is more important than its content. When a lad, made suddenly aware of death, asks, "Is this the end or *is there more?*" his question is a poignant demand upon reality, important out of all proportion to his casual questions of yesterday. Or when the young girl, made suddenly apprehensive of the meaning of sex, cries out, "Does it have to happen to me?" someone must answer, someone in whom the dignity of the sexual basis of life has found sure moorings. A child's mood frequently turns a question into a confidence, and then the parent must answer whether he has the time or not. The very fact that he takes time for an answer may far outweigh the intellectual content of his response.

Nancy is exceedingly shy and sensitive under a would-be blasé thirteen-year-old sufficiency. In her course on medieval history she read the life of St. Francis and is imbued with the idea of adopting a life of voluntary poverty. She resolves that hereafter she will wear no better clothes, spend no more lunch money, have no more of anything than the poorest in her class can afford. She vows in her heart to let her friendliness toward all become her "radiant garment." This attitude is new to Nancy, who has from childhood evidenced a special flair for being well dressed and having things. After three or four abortive attempts to consult her mother about her new vow, she finally takes her courage in hand and speaks.

"Mother, how old must a person be to become a saint? Do you think that if a person gave up her worldly goods entirely that others would soon begin to see something different — something sort of glorious, you know — shining

around her?" Nancy is trembling beneath her casualness.
So much depends upon the answer.

But her mother misses the mood of the question entirely.
She is dressing to go out and in her haste she merely
laughs, not unkindly but with genuine amusement. "Nonsense, silly. We don't have saints these days. Whatever
put such a notion in your head?"

"But the idea is the same as it was back in St. Francis'
time," insists Nancy falteringly. "People still have need
and — and — you can't understand need unless you share
it. You can't understand hunger if you always have
enough to eat. Sometimes you have to be poor on purpose.
Don't you think so?" Nancy concludes lamely.

Now her mother's laugh has an edge of irritation.
"What on earth will you think of next?" She calls to
Nancy's father who is reading the newspaper in the next
room. "Daddy, listen to your daughter. She doesn't
think she's poor enough."

Among all Nancy's acquaintances, probably no one has
a kinder mother than her own. Nor a more generous one.
And yet in this instance her mother has not only been
ungenerous but callous. If exigencies of time absolutely
prohibited an answer at the moment when Nancy asked
the question, then her mother should have managed some
way to carry over both the mood and the question until
she could give adequate consideration.

"I know what you mean, Nancy," her mother might
have said. "Lets talk about it as soon as I come home from
this tea. Meet you here in my room where we won't be
interrupted. Don't forget, will you, because I have an idea
of my own that I'll tell you about if you promise not to
laugh."

"Oh, I won't laugh, Mother. Some of my ideas are kind
of — funny — too."

Whereupon Nancy goes off to do something else until her mother comes home. But she has not lost her eagerness, and the shyness is eased a bit. When her mother returns and really has time to talk, both are a little better prepared by the interim of "thinking it over." The delayed conversation is successful, however, only because her mother made an immediate and honest answer to the *mood* of Nancy's question.

Sometimes, of course, a mood cannot wait. The question may be a kind of confession, or a desperate need which blurts itself out at an unexpected moment. Then the parent puts aside his present occupation, no matter what it is, and answers the mood, thanking his lucky stars that there is a question to take hold of.

Parents face another difficulty, less apparent but more far reaching than the necessity for meeting every question with an answer. They discover that they cannot give answers larger than their own understanding, and yet that no answer is sufficient unless it points the way to larger understanding than the parent himself has. In an effort to appear more authoritative than he really is, a parent frequently overreaches himself and hence accomplishes nothing.

David, who knows that his father does not go to church, has been asking him what is meant by "the house of God." Does God live in the church? His father has told him that some people find God in church, but others find him in other places.

"Where do you find God, Daddy?"

"In nature," says his father mechanically. "Out in the woods listening to the birds 'each in his separate language.' Looking at the flowers. Walking under the stars."

David makes no comment. He is lost somewhere between memory and reason. For David has lived nine

years with his father and knows that his father cannot tell
the birds apart, except the sparrow and the robin. He
has gone walking with his father in the evening, but he
has never seen his father look up at the stars. David does
not put his contemplation into words, not even into clear
thoughts. He does not impugn his father's honesty. He
just fails to register the fact that his father finds God in
nature. His father had tried to give an answer larger
than his own actual experience and his words were meaningless.

Emily, whose mind is as quick and nimble as her little
brown fingers, brings home a red mark in language study.
She acknowledges that she failed because she did not learn
the fifty lines of poetry assigned to her grade.

"Emily Williamson," says her mother sternly, "it isn't
just that you could have learned those lines in an hour if
you had put your mind to it. It's that poetry is important. Poetry contains the best thoughts of the ages. I
certainly don't want a daughter of mine to grow up without real love of poetry."

Emily listens unmoved. Perhaps she is vaguely proud
of her mother's defense of poetry and she supposes that
her mother subscribes to the theory she has just set forth;
but Emily has never seen her mother pick up a book of
poetry when she wants to read something. Indeed, there
is no poetry in the house except books left over from her
parents' college days, and they are up on the highest shelf
of the bookcase which no one can reach. Her mother's
words are the belligerent defense of an ideal, and in that
sense they are honest, but the mother has never experienced
her ideal. Therefore her words, which might have been
seeds to bring forth harvest, lack vitality. For all that will
ever grow from them, they might as well be pebbles.

Naturally most parents are not deliberately trying to

deceive their children. Indeed, the very vehemence of their answers is frequently proof that thy are trying to impart a truth they have never experienced. Thus they may steadfastly affirm that the universe is friendly, though they have never found it so. Or they may protest broken homes, feeling the foundation slipping beneath their own. The intent of their answers is reassurance. They want to preserve for their children a few firm pillars which will not crumble in bad weather. But they confuse reiteration with genuine reinforcement. The end result is, of course, the same as if they had dedicated themselves to deception. It is simply an impossibility for a parent to give an answer larger than his own understanding. Nevertheless, a parent must somehow make plain to his child that the final answer to any question is probably larger than the parent's own experience or understanding.

Answering questions would be easier if the child could accept the parent's judgment but he usually wants to try things out for himself. Moreover, while he has "to learn to live," at the same time, he needs to live as he learns. Many parents spend twenty-one years, or at least sixteen, getting their children ready to live, without ever realizing that they are living in childhood just as fully, probably, as they ever will. Unless they enjoy life as they go — relish each new day, savor each new experience, have a lively sense of adventure for each new task — the chances are not great that a sense of adequacy and elation will suddenly bloom within them when they are "grown up."

"I don't want to practice, Mummy," says Ethel, aged ten. "Why, yes you do, dear," says Mother cheerfully. "When you grow up, you'll love being able to play the piano."

Ethel shrugs her shoulders. That future day is too far off to matter. At the first opportunity she slips out to play.

That night her mother speaks to her father. "She'll be sorry when she's sixteen and the boys want to sing and she can't play for them. I know that when I got into high school, I was sorry I couldn't play the piano. I often told my mother that she should have made me practice whether I wanted to or not."

"Just tell her that if she can't practice, she can't play outdoors," says Ethel's father in his that-will-fix-her voice. "If I'm willing to pay for her lessons, the least she can do is to practice. I want her to have things I never had." He scowls as he opens his paper. When he was a boy he longed for a flute but his father could not afford the flute and his mother thought it made too much noise.

Both of Ethel's parents are right enough, as far as they go. The difficulty is that they forget that the child needs to enjoy her music *now*. She is living *now*. She is living a ten-year-old life just as fully as she will later live a twenty-year-old life. More fully, probably and alas, then she will live a forty-year-old life.

If a little girl is to understand what is meant by working for a future good, she has to have some element of experience through which to interpret the future. But most important is her enjoyment of her music in the present, for emotional appreciation of living is a habit just as truly as chromatic technique is a habit. No matter how high-priced her music teacher may be, how skillful, how devoted to her art, she is probably the wrong teacher for Ethel, because teachers teach joy in the doing or they do not really teach. And if they teach joy in the doing, then the pupil *is* living now. The years ahead may give Ethel greater understanding of her mother's interest, her father's support, her friends' appreciation, but joy in the doing will still be the primary quality which gives her music and her living its full zest.

Emil, half a dozen years older than Ethel, comes suddenly upon the realization that he lives as he learns. One day he is bending over a rowboat from which he has been scraping old paint preparatory to applying a new coat. Overhead stand tall pines with the sun splashing through their needles to make patterns on the waves which nibble at the shore. Suddenly Emil looks up from his work and speaks to his father who is mending the torn leather on an oar.

"A fellow doesn't mind this sort of work if he keeps his mind on next week when the boat will be finished and have the motor in it."

His father also looks up quickly but responds slowly. "What do you mean — 'next week'? Lots of us miss half the fun of living because we keep our eyes on tomorrow."

"Maybe that's so," says Emil, looking intently at the paint scraper while the idea soaks in.

His father smiles broadly. "My Cousin Becky now, she's that sort of procrastinator. She never will know that life's best tense is its present tense. Ever since I can remember, Becky's spent her spring in housecleaning in order to get ready for summer, her summer canning fruit and knitting sweaters to get ready for fall, the fall in preparing for winter and the winter in getting the family ready for spring. I've never seen her when she seemed to be enjoying her family now."

"Maybe being in a stew over what's coming next is her way of being happy."

"Nope," says his father, gesturing with his hammer. "She's always getting ready to be happy. Tomorrow is going to be a big day but today's joys pass her by."

"Maybe you're right," says Emil, again gazing intently at his scraper but seeing something far, far within his own spirit. "Maybe you're right."

"Now take us," his father persists. "The hour is pretty

swell just as it stands. Maybe there's an added quality in knowing that we'll have a big time when the boat is finished, but I doubt if we'll really have a better time than we're having right now."

Emil goes back to his work and — we have it from Emil — from that moment he had a greater zest for living, as if some one had pushed back a curtain and given his days new dimension.

Certainly one way to deepen a child's appreciation of living as he goes lies in helping him to master his tasks and their implements. No one, young or old, can feel up-and-up about life if he must constantly perform a task for which he has never acquired any skill, or use a piece of machinery of which he is afraid. He has to feel adequate. In so practical a matter as dishwashing, a little girl who learns to "clean and stack" thoroughly, and to wash from glassware and silver toward pots and pans, has an experience of organization and achievement which the child who dumps everything into the dishpan cannot know. In practical knowledge there is a distinct advantage in learning to cooperate with materials on their terms, for every kind of material has a law-of-itself, a law which becomes a handle, so to speak, when an individual wants to use it efficiently.

Take literal tools — saw, hammer, plane, brace, and bits. A hand-minded boy may ask how to use a plane but he is not going to ask how to take care of a plane, and the care is as much as part of the law of the plane as its cutting edge. Somehow a boy is poorer who has never experienced the law of tools, who has never resented with the axe the fact that someone has dropped it blade down against a stone, who has never rebelled with the saw at not being hung up properly. In tools there is integrity which approaches personality. They not only demand respect but must receive it, just as human individuals must, if they are to be useful to the point of their full stature.

And this is a point which a father has to impart to the child without the child's asking. Some of the most important questions are never asked but they have to be answered.

Raymond, who is ten, has gone to visit his grandparents in the country. The first week he learns to use a hammer and nails, the second he experiments with a small plane and the medium brace and bits. Finally he is given for his own a sharp little hatchet with which to whittle tent stakes for his new tent. After the tent is pitched, he goes back to work with hammer, nails, and saw as he builds his tent furniture. Suddenly one morning he needs the hatchet. His grandfather has been noting for several days that the hatchet is missing from Raymond's tool rack. He has admonished the boy over and over: "Check up on the tools, Ray. When you leave them for the night, leave them in their places. A good carpenter can't sleep when his tools aren't accounted for, any more than a good shepherd can close the fold with a lamb or two still straying."

"Sure," says Raymond absently.

And then the morning when he needs his hatchet. He hunts, and he finds it in the tall grass back of the tent. The hatchet is rusty. Although he understands that tools must not be allowed to rust, it has never really occurred to him to wonder why tools should not rust. Feeling vaguely guilty he begins to chop the kindling he wants for his campfire. The wood is hard and the hatchet is dull. He becomes exasperated. Indeed, he is thoroughly disgusted. He hunts his grandfather.

"This hatchet's no good, Grandfather. It won't cut. The hardware man gypped us."

His grandfather looks at the hatchet, feels its edge "The hardware man didn't gyp us. It was a fine little hatchet. But you've broken the law of the hatchet and both you and the hatchet pay the price."

Raymond looks ashamed. But he does need a hatchet. "Could I borrow your hatchet for a few minutes?"

"Sorry," says his grandfather "but it wouldn't be fair to my hatchet."

By the time Raymond's hatchet is cleaned and the edge reground, he has a different understanding of hatchets. He may not know any more about chopping but he has a new and more friendly relationship to his tool.

But there is a delicate point here, if a parent wants a child to be happy in using his skill, and that is for parent and child both to remember that tools are only tools. Because they need to be treated with integrity, for the sake of mastery, it does not follow that they have integrity in any moral sense. At best, they are *things*, and their demands are not to be confused with the demands and needs of persons. A boy who has been careless with an ax has been careless with a piece of steel and wood, the cost of which, to be sure, may be equated with someone's time and energy, but the ax has no growing personality to be stunted. It is the boy who has the personality, the character. Many times we become confused at this point and impute to the careless boy a moral weakness when actually he has a careless attitude toward tools — which may have small meaning or importance in his life as seen by him. We might see tools — and all sorts of *things* — in better perspective if tools came free and if we paid a fine for warping a boy. One way to keep the day-by-day joy in life free-flowing is to maintain this perspective between things and people.

One great reason for the success of the Boy Scouts

and like organizations lies in the thoroughness with which they answer what L. P. Jacks used to call the need for trusteeship, and at the same task help the young to enjoy their tasks. In a variety of interests the 4-H Clubs teach the same things: first, a knowledge of the elements necessary for development of a project, then responsibility for following the rules which bring full results; and all the time imparting zest for the doing.

To be a parent is to be perpetually discouraged, especially in moments of success because there are so few of them. The more clearly a parent discerns what it means to be a parent, the less he feels equal to the task, especially if he *is* equal to it. But fortunately, no matter how many our failures, even a successful parent may turn over a new leaf, glue it down, and stand on it smiling triumphantly. There are fresh, unwritten pages ahead.

II. Paradox for Parents

You parents all that children have,
And you too that have none,
If you would keep them safe abroad,
Pray keep them safe at home.

JANE AND ANN TAYLOR (*London*, 1662)

Most of us become parents before we have figured out exactly what the parent's part is in giving life and eventual maturity to new human beings. But of two things we are reasonably certain: We must make our children independent of our care and, in the process, we must give them sufficient security so that their growth will be sturdy and unhampered. Almost from the beginning of their lives we try to foster their independence. We teach them to crawl after their own toys, to stand on their own feet. We wean them not only from the mother's breast but from a thousand other dependencies upon us. We want them to wash their own hands, and eventually their necks and ears, to put away their own clothes and toys and books, to devise their own games, to do their own lessons, to make up their own minds. The weaning process is a long one extending from infancy through adolescence for the fortunate children whose parents are really determined to make them truly indpendent individuals. For the less fortunate, the weaning process may never be fully accomplished and they go through life tied by invisible strings to parents who have let the possessiveness of their love prove a fatal embarrassment to their children's maturity.

But all the time that we are fostering independence we are also trying to give them a sense of security. We want them to feel that we stand between them and the world. Whether it is a matter of untying hard knots in small shoelaces, or providing warm houses and good food, we are always devising ways to keep them from feeling overwhelmed by circumstance.

To manage the weaning process within a framework of security is difficult for a variety of reasons. The older generation tends to set standards in terms of the customs of yesterday while the new generation is trying to invent the folkways of tomorrow; the rules which one highly successful parent uses for one highly successful child may not work at all for his next child or for the neighbors' children; the rope which appears to tether one boy is sufficient to hang the next one; the alacrity with which one daughter copies her mother's manners and attitudes is matched by another daughter's flair for doing everything in exactly her own way. The entire parent-child relationship is such an individual affair that rule books seem to be more useful on the shelf than in the hand. And yet, of course, we all know that we have a heap of problems in common; that children are pretty much alike even when most appallingly different.

Certainly there are a few basic considerations which all parents have to meet or to ignore, which is just another way of meeting them. One such matter is the child's need for dependable responses to his conduct. His security lies in his being able to count on a fair degree of consistency in his emotional environment; this consistency is his home base from which he dares make independent sallies. How can he find his way in a universe which depends so largely upon law if the parents with whom he deals most intimately have one reaction on Tuesdays, when they are rested

and serene, and another reaction on Fridays, when they
have been up all night?

A kitchen stove, if it has a fire within, will burn the child
each time he makes the mistake of touching it. But the
child's mother has no such constancy of response. She probably scolds him for losing the dime with which he was to
buy a loaf of bread only if she really needs that loaf of
bread in a hurry. Otherwise she may give him another
dime and an absent-minded word of caution. She has no
law for lost dimes nor for scoldings. Or perhaps father
is the variable. One night he brings home a guest who
thinks it is "awfully cute" in little Junior to take the evening paper apart and spread it like a sidewalk down the full
length of the living room. But another night father comes
home without a guest and wants to read the paper immediately. On that night he thinks it disgraceful that a
three-year-old should not know enough to leave the
newspaper alone.

However, the point need not be labored to parents who
so often meet and mourn their own inconsistencies. Most
of us have a deep and poignant desire to deal fairly with
our children. Our inconsistencies burn secret scars.

The place is a summer cottage, the morning chill and
drizzly. Peg, the mother of four lively boys from eight
down, is dressing Peter, the four-year-old, who prances
and dances, slumps and wiggles, all in high glee touched
with defiance.

"Stand still!" says his mother sternly. "I have to get
you dressed right now." Peter continues to prance, standing on a chair.

"Peter do you hear me? You have to stand still and I
don't mean maybe." Bob, aged eight, slowly draws on a
sock. "He isn't listening."

"He'd better listen. Peter, don't you dare wiggle out
of your shirt again." Peter wiggles out.

At that point Grandmother comes in, sees the delay and suggests, "How about letting me dress Peter? Here, Peter, stand still while Grandmother dresses you."

Peter prances right on. His grandmother does mental sums. Should she really come down on the child as she would have done with his father? Or, since he is a guest in her home and she does want the children to think it a great treat to be there, should she worry through with him? Her voice shows her indecision. "Peter, Peter, can't you stand still?"

Then Great-grandmother comes in, takes in the situation, and says, "Breakfast's ready downstairs. Here, I'll dress Peter." She picks up the thrice castoff trousers. "Peter, stand still and put your foot in."

Peter looks at her, sharp blue eyes meeting blue eyes just as sharp. He stands still. Only his jabber goes on. In a moment he is dressed.

And then Bob speaks again. "Wasn't it funny the way Pete knew which one meant what she said?"

Maybe the older generation — the really older generation — had something in knowing their minds. Come meant *come* and go meant *go* and a child knew where he stood. Nowadays we say, "I wish the children would go to bed on time, but it just seems like . . ." We say, "I tell Jim to leave the hand scythe alone but of course he sees his father use it and so . . ." Or, "I told Polly three times she couldn't spend another nickel on the Good Humor man, but she knows that if she keeps teasing and all the other children . . ." Or, "I declare, they just wear you down till I wonder why we ever say no in the first place." And, "I gave in last time so she thinks I'll give in again." Thinks? She knows.

How can children find their way among the mind-changings of their parents? Nothing is for sure; no means maybe; yes means just don't bother me. Why, then, should a red light at a crossing mean *stop* — and no arguments? Why should not a road sign, *no passing*, mean go ahead and pass if you can get away with it? Must the child be always tugging at the law to see how much it will give to his whim? Really, children deserve better at our hands. They deserve the security of an honest yea and nay.

If someone walked up to us and said, "My dear, you're a jolly mother but a terrific liar," we would resent the accusation. "Me? Tell a falsehood? One thing I respect is the truth. I wouldn't fib the least three months off Nellie's age in order to take her to California on a half-fare ticket." But when we say, "Jack, be home at ten," what we mean is, "I wish I had time to think through this whole matter of night hours for junior high students, but it's just too hard to battle down arguments, so I'll say ten and maybe he'll really get in by eleven-thirty." He understands! So then, a year or two later, when we say, "No drinking," and "No fast driving," our young translate our admonitions into the coin they are used to handling. There is a Gresham's law for words as well as for money and our cheap counterfeit for decision drives out integrity.

Actually children thrive on firmness. They ask for it. Not in words but in the questioning which lies beneath words. Not for harshness; not unreasonableness; not pre-emptory orders. But a thought-out *yes* and *no* which can stand on firm feet and not melt down under siege. As a matter of fact, parents who mean what they say are not besieged. Children know when to save their breath. Children know when to respect a fence. And thy kick up their heels much more happily inside fences. They need the security of limitation. As they grow older the posts can be moved back to give them more room; indeed, the adolescents themselves may help to stake out the moveable fence — set the coming home time, decide on the allowance — but the fence indicates that their parents have an eye to their well-being and do not ask them to be responsible for too much territory. It's a dilemma — how much rope and how much roaming. But it is a dilemma for parents to meet with honest decision, and having arrived at a conclusion to speak the dependable word.

A second contribution the home may make toward security and independence is development of a sense of organization in the child. A fine phrase and a noble aim, we admit as soon as we hear the word, but in this cluttered, cumbered world what is a sense of organization? We ask the question in a tone that may range from irony to despair. It is all very well for columnists and psychiatrists to talk about the well-knit personality but most of us feel we were subject to drop-stitches in our own childhood and have been raveling ever since. We know that the well-organized individual is supposed to plan ahead, and not take on more than he can carry, and budget his time, energy, and other resources; not to let himself be short-changed on fun and leisure; never to neglect his health; to carry his work with verve, display resourcefulness in crisis, have an unfailing sense of humor — meaning proportion — and keep the bills paid. We realize that an individual with a sense of organization never gets the cart before the horse, the spending before the saving, the picnic before the vacuum cleaning, the earrings before the raincoat. He knows where he is going and what he is going to do when he gets there — and even why he went. That's fine, that's jolly, that's all very commendable. But he probably has a different kind of husband than we have, or a different wife, or maybe one of each. If he had to catch the commuters' special at seven-ten the year around . . . if he had to get the three children off to school while feeding the baby and dodging Junior's Wild West bullets so he won't think he's playing alone . . . if he had to give something to everything that doesn't make the Community Chest and save the newspapers, bottles, stamps off letters, Indian pennies, old spools, nylon hose with runs, and soap wrappers for other collectors . . . if he had a microscopic utility room instead of a basement and attic, and a shopping bag instead of a garden — or a garden instead of a shopping bag — but that's the way it *is*. And still parents are supposed to pass on a sense of organization. Well, that's the dilemma of it, spelled with seven letters or four. That's the parents' answer to the child's cry for self-assurance in an unsure world.

One old-fashioned concomitant of organization is order, the garden-variety everything-in-its-place kind. Instituting order is an all-family job, although one parent has to turn on the ignition and it helps when father's at the wheel. But when a family catches on that order is an inner-peace kind of security and a time-saving provider of independence, then it is amazing how inventive old and young can become in finding places and demanding co-operation. Every member of the family with at least a mite of dresser space, desk space, treasure space; plenty of closet hooks, high and low; a spot for school books, a box for toys, a place for wrapping paper and string, a wall for tools to hang on, a rack for socks to dry on, a couch which the young may pile on. Ingenuity is the big word. And then a fine for every "Where's my . . ." if it's where the owner left it, and a bigger fine for the one who did not replace it. If a child is accustomed to finding his undershirts in Mother's dresser drawer one week, among Daddy's socks the next week, on the back stairs the third week, let him have a drawer of his own and see with what relief he turns to it. To be sure, he may not turn instantly because he is a creature of habit. Not only Rome but the Romans took more than a day abuilding. But a parent may be shocked to observe with what alacrity and what relaxation children adjust themselves to an ordered environment, especially when the order includes a dependable schedule of meals and sleep. The young can be seen visibly to gather themselves together.

Naturally families differ in their patterns of order. One individual, looking back, says: "In my father's house, the furniture stood in the same place for fifty years. I could get up in the night and no matter how dark it was, I knew where each chair stood in the living room. In the kitchen I could reach for the salt or the vinegar and mix a gargle in the dark as well as if the light were on." But another may recall: "When we went off to school in the morning, we never knew how we would find the furniture when we came home at noon. Mother loved to change things around and could make that old parlor look like forty different rooms."

At first glance it may appear that the household which never moved the furniture was the one which made the greatest contribution toward security. But in the second household, although the order kept changing, there was still order. In both cases the children of the household felt that things belonged in place. And in both cases, order was not an end in itself. It cannot be an end in itself if it is to produce a liberated and competent personality; it must be balanced against other family needs.

But environmental order is only one aspect of organization. Children are not born with an inner knowledge of the way to keep up their school work, do their errands, manage their household tasks, get in their favorite television programs, practice their band instrument and still get nine hours sleep. The deal takes planning. And not plan-

ning *for* but planning *with* the child. If he can tell time
and write figures, he can draft a time budget. Help him
to make it roomy. Be free with the unaccounted-for
quarter-hours. And leave some beautiful white space,
indicative of doing-as-one-pleases. But no matter how
generous and genial the time budget, its purpose remains
organization. It is the outward and visible reminder of
an inward orientation between the self and circumstance.

Attitudes toward money have a profound effect on a
well-organized life. Children begin early to ask adjustment to money. Their first questions are likely to be the
gimme variety. And parents' answers tend to swing between unmotivated generosity and unintelligent recrimination. Money is energy, life, work application, a symbol of
honor and *noblesse oblige*. The sooner a child learns to
treat it with respect, but not awe, the firmer he stands in
relationship to other of his growing responsibilities. Saving
is a great habit and mighty few children oversave, but giving is a great habit too, and a lot harder to activate with a
sense of proportion. Just by virtue of being born into a
family a child deserves a share of the family income, not
only as spent by the parents for his basic upkeep, but to
spend himself for such items of upkeep as fall within his
judgment span. And the dependability of his judgment,
once he sees the whole picture and his place in it would
surprise many a male parent. Beyond his equitable share,
a child also deserves a chance to make money on a sound
basis, whether by the good old newspaper route or by
performing such extra tasks as paid help might otherwise
perform. Nevertheless, earning his way can be an over
emphasized virtue along with untying the knots in the
string on packages. Time has values beyond the mone-
tary, and the interrogative *when* is quite as important as
how much in regard to earning.

A sense of organization has a pleasant way of spreading, clover-fashion, so that in time it takes over the ground. Then both parent and child can feel secure about a new growth of independence.

No matter what the excellencies of his environment, however, nor the soundness of his habits, no child can feel secure nor yet independent if he is hounded by fear. Few of us who are adult realize how many and how deep are the fears of seemingly well-adjusted children. And one reason we do not see their fears is because we are pre-occupied with our own. In general, a fear of lostness haunts us; financial, cultural, social, political, spiritual lost-ness.

But we do think we keep our fears from our children. We say "I'm worried to death for fear John will lose his job in the merger, but I don't mention it before the chil-dren." "I'm afraid the landlord is going to sell this house but I haven't mentioned it to the children because they'd collapse if they thought they had to move out of the neighborhood." "I'm afraid John's uncle will have to come live with us but I haven't breathed it to the children." "I worry about Karen's orthodenture, but I wouldn't want her to know we can't afford it." "I'm afraid my eyes are going bad but I wouldn't want the children to know." Noble us, being fearful all alone. As if we didn't convey our anxieties in the tones of our voice, in our quick, nervous movement, in our trigger responses to small an-noyances. It is impossible for the most strong-minded to keep his fears to himself, and parents are seldom strong-minded at home.

Not only do children pick up the fears of their elders, in mood if not in detail, but they have an accumulation of their own. Often we fail to recognize that the child who seems short-memoried by day is long-memoried by night, or in the recesses of his own uncertain mind. A fear does not have to be vocal, or even legitimate, to be devastating. And it is just because we see the ridiculousness of a child's fear that we may not take in that it is a security-robbing experience. Or that it operates to short-circuit his independence.

In general children are subject to two kinds of fear, fear of imaginary danger and fear of real danger. Or is all fear fundamentally imaginary, just a failure to appraise reality and muster resources? The answer depends upon one's cosmology, one's scheme of meaning in the universe, one's understanding of who he is and where he is going. Certainly among young children more than half the fear is of imagined danger, largely fear derived from their reaction to comic books, to radio and television programs, and to the loose talk of their elders.

After Alfred, nine and a precocious reader, has lain awake four consecutive nights afraid that the Terrorist will step out of his clothes closet, knife in hand, his father takes over the comic-book situation. He scrutinizes the entire household accumulation, including the maid's books. Finally he decides that the only way to root out the fear is to root out the cause of the fear. Answering a child's need can sometimes be just that drastic, but Alfred's father scarcely realizes how socially involved a fear can be. He decrees which books can be Alfred's fare and tries to mollify his incensed offspring by subscribing to two series which come magazine-fashion each month. The rest are taboo — and no argument.

A sullen Alfred rebels; his hair-raising favorites are missing. "I can read them at Johnny's," he says. "You'll never know. Johnny's father doesn't care."

"It's true I can't police the houses of the other boys,"

his father agrees. "But I expect you to abide by the standards of the family."

Being an honorable child and feeling cornered, Alfred wails, "But look-ut the money I've spent for comic books."

"Tell you what," says his father, "I'll buy up your comic books and burn them."

So Alfred rounds up his books and his father pays cash. Next day Alfred brings more books; his father pays more cash. The third day another twenty.

"There couldn't be that many comic books in one house," his father expostulates.

"Of course not," Alfred agrees. "But I thought if you wanted to clean up on me, you'd be glad to buy from the other kids, too. These are the ones they don't need any more."

His father makes short halt of the racket, but he keeps his eye on the comic-book situation and on the matter of substitute occupations and books worth reading. He rouses himself. (That is often the way with freeing a child from fear: it discloses a need which may have ramification.) He goes to PTA and finds there are other parents who feel the way he does but have not yet taken a stand. A survey is instituted, parents reporting on the comic-book collections in their own bailiwicks. They confer with teachers who know well the subtle relationship of comic books to homework and recognize the personality marks of the fear engendered by the grotesque characters and fascinating tortures of the strips which hold the children under a spell.

However, the reforming fathers run into a snag in the form of the popular handcraft teacher, a young man with a collection of his own. He believes in rugged comic books. "Let the kids learn what kind of world they're living in.

Nobody draws a cartoon meaner than some people. I know. I went through the war in the South Pacific. The cruelest you can think up, that's what some fellow is ready to do to you."

One father wants to get the teacher fired. "He tells atrocity stories to the children in his woodworking class."

Alfred's father goes at it a different way and in the end wins a co-worker—Alfred gets interested in his father's clean-up on comic books and adds a couple of fertile ideas of his own, for a crusade at hand seems more exciting than a comic-book war among monsters from far places. It was excitement Alfred wanted in the first place; something big to identify himself with. Freed of his fear of imaginary terrors, he takes an interest in the firsthand events of the day. And no longer thinks twice about walking two blocks after dark to see his grandparents.

Radio and television, two of the children's best friends, can also be the enemy of sleep and the foster-parent of fear. Millie is a nurse in an excellent hospital. She is thirty-three, married, has two children and a husband who works nights. One morning she comes on duty late, makes two minor mistakes in administering medicines, drops a tray of thermometers. Then she blurts to a patient, "I was up all night with Helen. She's eleven and she glues herself to programs which scare her to death. Then she gets a nightmare and wakens hysterical and it takes hours to get her quiet."

"What about snapping off the program? After all, there is a switch."

"I tried that. I even had the repairman take out a piece and say the set was broken, but she just went to the neighbors. And anyway, sometimes I'm on duty till midnight."

"Can't you give her something else to do, and explain

that she'll have to abide by your decision about programs until she's older?"

Millie looks at her patient, obviously a well-educated woman for her bedside table was filled with books. "Look, dearie, you read a lot but maybe you never had children. *You can't buck the system.* Television's in. If Helen scares herself to death, there's nothing I can do."

There might be one or two things, in the interest of psychological security. Such things as protecting the child from her own immature judgment, and hence her fear, by observing the programs, taking a stand at home, and making one's views known to the sponsor and station. After all, public opinion is formed by the public of which each adult is a member. And determined parents have tremendous allies, usually, in the teachers, for teachers know the relationship of over addiction to television and radio to school work, to general alertness, even to health.

Beside the fear generated by the things children read and watch, there is also the fear which originates in loose talk, *loose* meaning unbridled, unproctored, without attention to small ears. "For every kind of animal and bird, reptile and sea creature, can be tamed and has been tamed by man . . . but no human being can tame the tongue." Not many, anyway; not when there is scandal or danger to report. But, we say, terrible things can happen to a child. A mad dog, a mad wind or a mad man is no respector of persons. Children have suffered these dire fates that make headlines. They have indeed. So let us be realistic in warning a child when he should be warned, but let us also learn to hold our tongues when silence saves a child from needless fear.

But is there not knowledge of facts and conditions which truly menace a child's security? Are there not

threats of which a child cannot help but be afraid? Take
the atom bomb. The shadow cast at Hiroshima falls across
the youngest in our bright land. Before a child goes to
school he knows that one H-bomb can annihilate his
home, his family, his city, himself. He knows about bomb
shelters and air raid drills. Isn't it better that he should be
forewarned even though awareness makes him fearful?

Harry, in the third grade, begins to bite his nails. He
never used to bite his nails. Moreover, there are blue cir-
cles under his eyes. He isn't sleeping well. His mother
thinks he plays too hard; his father feels he has worms.
One night as he is undressing he starts talking rapidly about
a strange dog which was killed by a car and then blurts out,
to his mother, "You'll have to carry the baby, and Daddy
will have Phil and Bill because they're twins and can hardly walk, but nobody will have me because I'm big."

"Carry them where?" asks his mystified mother.

"To a shelter when the bomb comes. We won't know
it's coming. They'll take us by surprise. Their plane
sounds just like any other plane. I'll be playing ball outside and I won't even look up. Even when the bomb hits
we won't know what happened for a minute. And if it
lands on us we'll never know. Then pretty soon the
houses will fall down inside and they'll burst into flames
and everybody will be running and you'll have the baby
and nobody will have me."

"Nonsense," says his mother shortly. "First off, there
isn't going to be any bomb. And second, if it comes the
way you say, there won't be any use running for a bomb
shelter. It will already be too late." Her tone brightens.
"When our house starts to burn, you and I'll grab fire
extinguishers. We'll put out the fire. And Daddy will
come home and say it wasn't really a bomb. It was just
an explosion in one of the big city gas tanks that started

some fires. Nobody was killed. The workmen were all home for lunch. Here, put on your pajamas."

Harry doesn't move. Only his fear is moving — underground. His fear is saying, "She's a cheerful nitwit. We'll hide from her but we'll talk again. We know this terrible thing will happen all right. Sooner or later it will happen."

Just then Harry's father comes upstairs. He looks into the room. Noting Harry's stark little face and the quick biting of his nails, he says, "What are you doing? Quit biting those nails."

Harry jumps. He jumps too hard; he practically dodges. His father sees that something is the matter; something is worrying the child.

"What's eating you?" he asks, sitting down on the side of the bed.

So Mother laughs and tells about the bomb. But Harry's father doesn't laugh. He says to her, "Harry could be right, you know."

"Do you want to scare him to death?" his wife asks, with a raising of eyebrows.

"No," Harry's father says shortly. "I want to show him how to live in an atomic age."

So then he explains a little of what it means to split an atom. He tells in general how bombs are made, and explains about every country's knowing that the use of bombs would bring retaliation which would mean mutual destruction. Even though he sometimes uses a big word, Harry's small ears and wide eyes quite take in what is being said. His father talks about the peacetime use of atomic energy, a thing no one had ever thought to mention to this third-grader. He talks about working for peace by sharing our abundance of food and technical knowledge and helping everybody's child to grow up without hunger or fear. Everybody's? Yes, all children everywhere, no matter what kind of government their country may have, because forms of government change, but people are much alike, at heart, everywhere. He talks way past Harry's bedtime.

When the talk is all finished Harry sighs deeply. For once he has no more questions. His father has not made out that the world is all right; not at all. But he's made out that the people in the world want it to be all right, most of them. And that they have a chance to make it all right. That's a job every individual should work at, beginning in any little old spot where he happens to be. In two minutes flat Harry is asleep. In the next few weeks he bites his nails only once in awhile when he gets excited or mad; then one day he realizes he doesn't bite them any more. After that, also, whenever Harry's mother or father read in a newspaper about constructive uses of atomic power, they happen to mention it at the dinner table.

Along with insecurity fostered by fear of the implications of the atom bomb is the more immediate insecurity, for many teen-agers, of entering the armed forces. Some see their stint merely as time to serve, seldom dwelling on the possibility of fighting. Some anticipate with excitement the freedom from home restrictions, a chance to see the world. Some try not to think about their turn; something may happen to avert it. Some feel they should not co-operate with an organized program of warfare. A few know they cannot. But all realize they are about to be shaken loose from their accustomed pattern; deflected from their main course.

And not only boys experience frustration in the delay to their career caused by "the draft." Girls realize that their lives are tied in with their brothers and boyfriends. Some look at the two-year hitch as a time of waiting for their man to come back; some fear the waiting, fear their own capacity to change, and their man's. Some enter the armed forces themselves. Some are pacifist to the bone and bewilder their boyfriends with the ardor of their arguments. As with the boys, fear is overlaid with other emotions and attitudes and comes to the surface obliquely.

While not all teen-agers duplicate the thought pattern of their parents by any means, still the attitude of the young toward war follows the main lines of the adult generation. The proportion of students who adhere to the principle of nonparticipation in, or preparation for, war is larger than the proportion of parents, but when their call comes, the pressure of circumstance usually maneuvers the young into line. Not, of course, without considerable neurosis which may or may not come to the surface later. It is a delicate matter to gauge the extent to which boys do violence to their conduct-judging mechanism by being pressured into a course of action which runs counter to standards of reverence for life, respect for personality, constructive use of time, and many other ideals which society has endeavored to build into them. The deep mind, at whatever layer of consciousness judgments are assembled and sorted, is bound to register confusion so that future actions becomes increasingly hard to appraise, especially when the dictates of conscience go contrary to social judgment.

How can an ordinary parent of us answer these fears which assail our children at various age levels? How can we deal with individual fears which are the product of a social situation? How shall we answer the vast uncertainties which seem contingent upon the state of our world? It would be easier, no doubt, if the young could bring their uncertainties to the surface in overt questions, but one earmark of fear is its proclivity to stay underground — as if in not being faced it denied its own reality. Hence we are always having to answer questions which are not asked.

Our primary answer to the fears of the young is to share our own freedom from fear. But this kind of support is only possible to the degree that we are actually without fear. And how do we, tangled in our years of fears, ever get free enough of them to be of use to our children?

First, no doubt by realizing that fear defeats its purposes. Even at the physiological level it reacts against us, shooting an oversupply of adrenalin into our system along with named and unnamed hormones, upsetting both endocrine balance and blood chemistry, affecting the permeability of the cell walls and instigating other deleterious changes. The short of it is that long-run fear jams the works! Our children may not understand the attrition of fear wearing us to subnormal efficiency but they bear the brunt of our fear-born shortened tempers. They seldom realize, "My father is afraid; that's why he barks so," or "My mother is devoured by fear; that's why she has headaches and backaches and never goes out," but they react to our fears in their own ambivalences.

At the psychological level fear makes us want to bind all our tomorrows within today's limitations, leaving nothing to the inventiveness and courage of the days to come. Fear paralyzes our judgment, short-circuits our resourcefulness, saps our mental verve. And at the spiritual level it is the great denial; for practical purposes it negates God. Now we know these things as well as the next person. We are quick enough to tell a neighbor that fear never held at bay a wolf, a mortgage, an epidemic, or a war. It never averted a typhoon or a depression. Or a family argument. We acknowledge that although the human race learns slowly, it would seem as if by this time we could get along without witches' spells, asafeida bags, chastity belts, battering rams, and fears — all the antiquated methods of dealing with threatening circumstance.

In dealing with our children's fears we are sometimes able to get at our own more realistically, to lift them into the open, spread them out in the bright light of reason—our own, if you please—let the wind of common sense blow through them, and then deal with them one by one. After which we can sit down by the kitchen table and pray devoutly, "Thank you, dear God, for endowing me with more sense than I thought I had, and other people with more co-operation than I thought they had, and for making more of your own strength available than I knew you had. Amen."

Perspective is a great stabilizer for parental fears. To look back at the fears of our fathers as reflected in their private and public arguments is to laugh off many of our own anxieties about our times. Our fathers were afraid of the disappearing frontier, of free silver, the Spaniards in Cuba, parcel post, subsidy of railroads, local option, votes for women, the power of the League of Nations, malaria rising from swamps, and of exhausting the national coal supply and being left without fuel. Stranger, they were sometimes fearful lest their own children might not prove the paragons they dreamed us to be. Against the sounding board of current affairs their fears have a weak reverberation. And so will our fears have a hollow rattle in the ears of our children. Is there not some way to teach a child to recognize the rattle before he is bit by the fear?

Quite a steep and winding road which parents travel. If at times it seems beset with hazards which trip us up so that we lose our balance, if not indeed our sense of direction, there is comfort in remembering that many generations have traveled the same difficult and exciting journey, parrying their paradoxes as they climbed.

III. The Child's World

How like an angel came I down!
How bright are all things here!
When first among His works I did appear,
O how their glory did me crown!
The world resembled His eternity,
In which my soul did walk;
And everything that I did see
Did with me talk.

THOMAS TRAHERNE (1633-1674)

Every parent knows that no two children live in the same world. Even though they are born into the same family under relatively similar circumstances, their worlds may be as different as if they had been born centuries apart or lived on different continents. Some of the difference lies in their native ability; that is, some are born smarter than others, with a greater natural ability for comprehension and adjustment. We say, "There is a difference in their genes," meaning, in our laymen's fashion, that some inherit a better endowment. Any geneticist will make plain that there isn't much that can be done about an individual's endowment. That is, after he is born. Society might do a great deal about producing better endowed individuals if enough people understood the importance of wise mating and then accepted the discipline of mating wisely. At present some 25 per cent of each generation gives rise to 50 per cent of the next generation, and not on a selective basis; the general tendency is said to be displacement of the best by the worse. However, the trend may change in this country with this generation of adults, as more sound middle-class parents of good physical inheritance and adequate economic underpinning are deliberately having larger families, while a larger proportion of the less desirable stock are taking advantage of knowledge about birth control.

A child appears to be born with a given capacity for intelligence. Improved environment can raise that intelligence somewhat, but only to a limited degree, a range of perhaps twenty points. Studies of identical twins are one of the criteria for determining what can be done within this range. Identical twin girls, for instance, separated at birth, brought up in different environments, show that the one who lacked opportunity, who quit school in the third grade and thereafter had no advantages, tested an intelligence quotient of 80, while her sister who had a normal school education and a better home environment tested 100, which is the standard known as normal intelligence. Moron to normalcy all because of training. A variance of twenty points may not seem much but if the capacity of all the people in any community could be raised one-fifth, the difference in community life would be considerable.

Another factor of native equipment which helps to condition the kind of world a child will respond to and make his own is his constitutional type. Commonly we say that some children are thin, some fat; some heavy boned, some fragile in bony structure; some are well-muscled, others scarcely muscled at all; some round in contour, some linear. Some have small stomachs, literally, some large; some have more than ordinary amount of gut; others have exposed nerves scarcely padded with fat.

Moreover, children are not round or well-muscled or angular in the same degree; constitutional types are mixed. But they can be measured morphologically so that it is possible for a parent to know rather exactly with what type of child he is dealing. This basic measurement or appraisal is called the child's somatotype ("*soma*" meaning "body.") And his somatotype varies little throughout his life, even though he may gain or lose flesh.

Furthermore, constitutional psychologists have found that certain temperaments are closely tied in with given somatotypes, so that when a child is measured, and his somatotype drawn up, the specialist can predict what diseases he is likely to have, whether he will be good in certain sports, clever with certain skills, whether he will hide when grieved or plunge into activity, whether he will respond to horses or shy away from them, whether he will prefer a house hid among trees or set upon a hill, and a thousand other miscellany which go to make up any individual's life.

These are facts about which a parent may become informed and thereby find his job of parenting made much easier as well as more intelligent. He will then know, for instance, which child to protect from studying in a room where the radio is on, which to allow plenty of privacy, which to encourage in sports, which to encourage in reading in a quiet corner, not to mention the more important matters of encouraging the right aptitude, friendships, and marriage.

A major consideration in our culture is the matter of enabling a child to grow in *his* best way, rather than after the pattern which most of society approves; that is, the pattern of cheerful socialization, constant activity, drive for success in terms of fame and fortune. At times most of us belong to the type of parent who cannot bear to see an idle child. Perhaps impatience with our child's apparent idleness springs from the realization that our own tasks are never finished. Perhaps we unconsciously inherit the tradition that "Satan finds mischief for idle hands to do." Perhaps we feel that "doing is learning," or that the silent child will become "introverted," or that his inactivity reflects upon our lack of ingenuity. Or we may feel that noise and laughter and action are synonyms for happiness.

Young Herbert lying on the grass looking at nothing and apparently thinking about the same thing is a target for parental suggestions. "Herbert, did you finish piling the wood?" Herbert did. "Herbert did you do your practicing?" Yes, that too. "Herbert, why don't you read your book?" He doesn't want to. "Herbert, what are you thinking about?" Nothing, just as his mother thought. But by and by from Herbert, who has continued raptly to do nothing for an hour, comes this question: "Can ants if they hurry and do their work well ever be anything but ants? Will they be men someday?"

The child's world has, obviously, a factual and an imaginative aspect, an inner and an outer aspect. Even the wisest parent would be put to it to say which part of a child's life is without and which within. What is the boundary of "within"? One child phrased it, "I am bounded by my skin. Outside of my skin is not-me, but inside my skin I stay the same except for growing. The most important thing to me is everything that goes on inside my skin including my skin. Inside my skin I am the boss." To which astute remark many scientists would point out that "inside the skin" the individual is not the boss he thinks he is, for he can only partially regulate the body's constant change, its way of perpetually renewing itself, molecule by molecule. And psychologists would point out another thing which every parent knows, namely, that environmental factors can modify the mind's ability to comprehend, reason, imagine, remember, in spite of the set of the will. The only interior constant which appears to remain intact in spite of change is some kind of design-of-individuality, some form of organized energy, variously named, which appears to act according to a plan of itself. Certainly this design-of-individuality — call it core self or soul or whatever — is not an exterior factor.

A child often seems surprisingly aware of this inner constant which appears to appraise and assess those aspects of his nature, and of all nature, over which he knows he has some control by means of thought. He becomes absorbed in determining where he himself leaves off and other people's prerogatives begin — a process of defining himself. He constantly experiments, at conscious and subconscious levels, with his own attitudes, moods, reactions. The outer world of events and action no longer holds the center of his interest, except sporadically, because he finds his own imagination more productive of satisfaction. When we sense this semiwithdrawal from exterior affairs we say, "Lately Suzie seems to be living within herself," or "John is certainly absorbed in his inner world."

Sometimes the child asks questions about his inner discoveries and problems; sometimes he does not sense them clearly enough to become articulate. And often, of course, he is unaware of the connection between cause and effect, mood and action, imagination and reality. It is in this realm that the parent has to continue his most productive activity — answering questions which are not asked.

The most casual of us is aware of some of the factors which condition our child's inner world and its outward expression in the emotions and reactions he is currently displaying. Some have discovered that none of the conditioning factors under our parental control is more relevant than the food our child eats. To be sure, children seldom ask questions about food, except, "May I have some more?" or "Why do I have to eat that?" And when they do ask we seldom bother with much of an answer. We say, "It isn't good to stuff," or "It's good for you, that's why you're to eat it," or "My father saw to it that we cleaned our plates." But we put off becoming knowledgable about nutrition, partly because we feel that we feed our children well enough as it is, partly because we aren't that interested in nutrition, partly because we have too much else to be concerned about, and partly just because. But we have the word of the experts that our children's behavior problems — especially adolescents — are more often complicated by nutritional deficiencies than the average one of us realizes; or, for that matter, than the average physician, absorbed in curing our children's out-and-out illnesses, has time to deal with. It takes a specialized nutritionist to offer basic help, and few fields are more open to fads and fanaticisms than the field of nutrition.

Nevertheless, nutritionists seem agreed that high school boys and girls ordinarily eat far less protein than they need and consequently lack the indispensable amino acids which are the primary building materials. They are also almost sure to be short on the energy-providing B-complex, and lacking in others of the vitamins and minerals without which health cannot abound. How can it be otherwise when most of our foods are raised on inadequately fertilized soil, and shunted through a complex of dealers before they reach our kitchens? Most high school youngsters scorn breakfast so that instead of its being a high protein meal, the most important of the day, they skimp or skip. Then they eat a haphazard lunchroom midday meal, long on starches and sugars. All three meals are likely to lack sufficient of the mineral-providing vegetables, either because the individual has decided he does not care for vegetables or because they are cooked in too much water and the minerals dissolved in the water go down the drain instead of down the gullet. Most of the high school young are active in spurts, a state which could be avoided if they consumed enough protein. Because a boy's energy is low he folds up with a vast weariness just when he should be mowing the lawn or accomplishing other assigned tasks. His father probably remarks that he has energy enough when he wants to take off on his own pursuits, but actually the lassitude which overcomes him when he faces an uncongenial task is nearer his true energy level than the psychologically induced zest with which he dashes forth to tear around.

A parent who wants to dig for information as to what constitutes adequate nutrition may find herself — or in some families himself — rendering a larger service in solving emotional difficulties than if she — or he — took a graduate degree in counseling, or hired a psychiatrist to supervise the young variable who dominates the household. The young themselves are oddly co-operative about nutrition once they get the main idea and begin to feel a pick-up in energy and looks; they not only begin to ask leading questions but make intelligent suggestions. Indeed, none is more canny than the young in devising ways and means toward ends deemed worthy of patronage.

Sleep is the other major conditioner of the inner world, the world of emotions, over which parents have some supervision. And here children's questions are likely to be the petulant "Why should I go to bed so early?" or, at the other end of the line, "Why do I have to get up?" Mostly we do not answer their questions very satisfactorily because we do not know the answers. There seems to be no accepted explanation of sleep. What makes us sleep?

How, exactly, do we fall asleep? Do the organs of the body function in the same way when we are in the unconscious state? Where on earth, or in the universe, is our mind while we sleep? What, after all, are dreams? Adults can share a common curiosity with children at these points.

Psychologists seem agreed that when a person falls asleep something happens in the forebrain region of the brainstem called the thalamus, the center which also regulates body temperature and performs other important tasks. The ancient Egyptians, who were good anatomists, are said to have left considerable material on the thalamus as yet unevaluated by Western science. They felt that the true purpose of sleep was to allow the soul with its mind concomitant to be free for instruction or for service in behalf of others. A modern parent would sometimes be glad to have his child's soul instructed in sleep. Modern scientists are more inclined to favor muscle fatigue as one reason, or predisposing factor, for sleep. Perhaps the muscles controlling the sensory organs share in general fatigue and consequently refuse to operate the sense organs, whose inoperation then causes a state of suspended consciousness. If so, we have a clue for getting to sleep: cease to hear, smell, see, or otherwise exercise the senses. But can the brain give orders to the sense organs to cease operation? Apparently with some training it can. Relaxation also seems to have something to do with sleep, as any parent of a baby knows. The muscles hardest to relax, and perhaps more important to relax, are said to be those around the eyes — a possible argument for the adolescent's not studying right up to bedtime. The hardness and softness of the bed seems to make a difference in the length and quality of sleep, as do posture habits while sleeping, and amount of bodily movement.

It is known that during sleep the body temperature is lowered and the rate of basal metabolism reduced, indicating that less physical energy is being used so that body cells have a better chance to repair themselves. Experimentation has also shown that when the mind sternly instructs the body to recuperate during sleep, it often does a more co-operative job. On the other hand, if for some reason it seems important to the individual to remain ill — as, for instance, a child's need of attention — then the cells do not rebuild as efficiently during sleep.

One good way to answer a child's questions about sleep is to let him experiment. From a practical standpoint we know that we all have to sleep or die, but people vary in their toleration of lack of sleep. Any parent knows that children of the same age do not necessarily require the same amount of sleep. One-directional persons who know exactly what they want out of life and are on their way — a quality which shows up early in some children — seem to require less sleep than dispersed or diffused personalities. One characteristic of genius is said to be the ability to get along on little sleep, but not all who need little sleep are geniuses; and few of the myriads of children who think they need little sleep are geniuses. Sometimes it helps to answer a child's questions about sleep to let him try a month of hit-or-miss and then a month of regularity. Try ten hours, nine, and so down the line until he finds his own best amount of sleep. Treated with intelligence children often act with intelligence!

Perhaps the parent's best answer anent sleep is the time-worn one that if we want to understand ourselves we have to deal with facts arrived at by open-minded observation, neither child nor parent trying to prove a theory of sleep, but watching, recording, and concluding. Young and old,

we are all in the same physiological boat, needing an em-
pirical chart and compass in order to make our way against
the current headwinds of modern civilization, or merely
to survive the doldrums of ignorance. Exasperatingly the
chart and compass often have to be mastered en route.

Exercise is no doubt a conditioner of the inner world
also, as parents soon discover when a reading-mad youngster insists upon sitting by the fire with a book while the
rest of the neighborhood slides and skates. The child who
never gets his blood up, as our elders used to say, is likely
to occupy himself increasingly with his inner world. On
the other hand, the child who is constantly involved in
adjustment to his outer world by way of muscular participation is likely to remain ignorant of the delights and uses
of his inner world. Since our culture puts a premium upon
athletic prowess and general sociability, outturned children
are more likely to ride with the tide. Here again the child
can find out for himself, under a bit of well-timed nudging,
that some exercise makes him feel better, or that some
measure of inward appraisal makes life easier to live.

Since the *self* and its whole inner world is so much at
the mercy of the body's well-being it seems a pity that
children cannot learn more about co-operating with the
body's laws; they learn other matters much more difficult
of comprehension.

This incident happened long enough ago so that its
significance in results can now be appraised. Two seven-
year-old boys in the same neighborhood had rheumatic
fever. The father of Howard was a physician, the father
of Ben a teacher. Both boys were very ill and both had
heart involvements which required long weeks of lying in
bed.

Howard's father said sternly to his son, "Howard, you

must not sit up. Not for any occasion." And to the boy's mother: "You'll have to keep watch of him because even one infringement could be serious."

Ben's father, repeating the doctor's orders, said to his son, "Bennie, you must not sit up. No matter what you want nor how badly you want it, you must not sit up even once." And to the boy's mother he said, "No child of seven can remember this sort of command unless he has some understanding of it."

Ben's mother, feeling her skill as an inculcator of obedience in question, rose on her dignity and said, "If I tell him not to sit up, he will not sit up."

Ben's father said, "Shucks!"

And then he set to work with his son. The acute illness was passed and the long convalescence lay ahead. He sat by the bed with pencil and paper and drew a picture of a heart, naming its four rooms after their proper nomenclature. Bennie liked repeating "ventricle" and "auricle"; and to think he had two of each! Then his father's pencil added long twisty pipes leading into and out of the heart, and these he called "veins" and "arteries." With the picture before him, Father told Ben a story about the heart's really being a pump which works day and night no matter whether its owner is waking or sleeping. The story amused Ben. It was different from the other kinds of stories he knew. He went off to sleep feeling rather comforted that he had such a dependable heart inside his chest.

Day after day, Ben learned new things about the pictures his father drew. The daily "lessons," which Ben did not know were lessons, lasted only a few minutes. Unconsciously he was picking up a new vocabulary and asking intelligent questions. One afternoon when he was decidedly getting better, his father brought home some charts, great, beautiful charts as large as a man himself.

They stood on a rack at the foot of Ben's bed. One was marked "The Circulatory System." Ben's twelve-year-old sister Evelyn thought the chart was exceedingly intricate but Ben himself thought it quite plain. By this time he understood in a general way how it was with a heart. The law of resting the heart in acute myocarditis seemed a reasonable law when you considered what a heart had to do.

Unfortunately Ben was known for his huge appetite. Before his illness, it was the marvel of all the cousins how he could eat so much and grow so fast. As soon as he was genuinely getting better this large hunger returned, although he was lying in bed and having no exercise except gentle massage. Sometimes he wanted to eat even more than he wanted to get well. The many little meals which came his way seemed like nothing at all. Then his father drew pictures of the digestive system. In two weeks Ben was talking glibly of chyle and chyme and confounding Evelyn with remarks about the cardiac orific and the pyloric orifice. By that time he understood why too full a stomach was hard on a tired heart. If the doctor said, "Five small meals each day," then five meals it was. Since he was a child interested in himself it would have been easy to give him an unhealthy preoccupation with his own internal mechanisms. But the physiology lessons were really only a very small part of his day along with color books, sets of pictures, guppie fish, the canary, and many naps.

One day Ben's mother went to call on Howard's mother. They had never been close friends but their mutual problem drew them together. Howard's mother looked ten years older. Howard would not stay flat in bed. He popped up for this and he popped up for that. He had made small progress in ten long weeks. The doctor-father was discouraged, Howard was irritable and his mother worn out. Very tactfully, Ben's mother told about the physiology lessons but Howard's mother said, "Howard wouldn't be interested in things like that."

After twenty-one weeks in bed, Ben began to get up and move about. When summer came he went to the woods where he swam a little and exercised heedfully. The next fall he started school, under mild restrictions. After thirty weeks, Howard was taken to the seaside with a nurse. At the end of a year he was up and playing some but was not in school. Every time he was really getting better and felt well, he ran too hard and lost the ground he had gained. Today there is exactly the difference between the health of the two boys which one would expect to find.

The moral of a layman's story can be easily overdone. There may have been other factors in the two cases than those which meet the eye. But the conclusion remains valid enough to be written large across the heavens which shelter parents: To answer as fully as we can a child's questions about his own physiology is to increase his respect for his body, to enable him to co-operate intelligently with nature, and — perhaps most important of all — to help him feel master of his own necessities. It is at this point of understanding and controlling the physical desires and preferences that the inner world of values and long-runs comes sharply against the demand for immediate satisfactions. Therefore a foresighted parent is forever pointing to necessities which become disciplines in the old meaning of the word, assisting the child to master himself so that he will be less at the mercy of circumstance. Fairly young children can learn with satisfaction the way in which environment impinges on the mind and controls the emotions — although not in these terms!

Fairly young children can learn with satisfaction the way in which environment impinges on the mind and conditions the emotions — although not in these terms!

"Why am I so crabby today?" asks Lucille suddenly, with complete ten-year-old candor.

"That's what I'd like to know," says her mother. She thinks a minute. "It may be because you were up so late last night."

"That couldn't have made me crabby because I had such a good time."

"But when you don't get enough sleep, then you're tired inside, no matter how good a time you had," says Mother. "Your stomach is a little tired, your liver is a little tired, even your feet are a little tired and hate to run errands. Maybe you don't *feel* tired because you are still excited about the company, but on the inside you *are* tired. And the reason you object with words every time you're asked to move is because your body is objecting inside you."

"Then why do you ask me to move?"

"The day's work has to go on. It wouldn't be fair to throw the whole family off schedule because you don't want to go buy a loaf of bread. The real point is that both you and I will remember after this that it pays to go to bed on time."

Lucille accepts the explanation with apparent indifference but the answer is not entirely wasted for on another day she comes to her mother to say: "Last night I wasn't up too late. But today I feel like disobeying everybody. What makes me that way?"

Mother thinks again. "Did you drink your orange juice for breakfast? Did you sleep well? Did you remember to go to the bathroom before you went to school?"

Lucille has a perfect record.

Mother keeps on trying. "Did you know your lessons? Did you get along well with the other children? Did anyone make you mad, or did you upset anyone else?"

Again Lucille seems to have a perfect record.

"Then I don't know why you feel so irritable," Mother acknowledges. "But there *is* a reason somewhere and we ought to be able to find it."

A little later Mother suggests, "Why don't you go up to your own room and read a little while?"

"Oh no," says Lucille. "I'm sick of that old room."

"Um," says Mother, and goes up to look at the room. There are Lucille's shoes, black and brown, for which her father had given her a shoe-shining outfit, thrown under the bed in need of a shine. There is her laundry bag full of the hose she is supposed to keep washed. In the bookcase, the books are upside down and backwards. Her desk is littered with scraps of paper used for arithmetic problems; her hairribbons dangle over the back of a chair. Nor is it any comfort to open the dresser drawers where handkerchiefs crowd socks in the place where only pajamas and undies belong. The week has been a very busy one for Mother and she has gone past Lucille's room hastily, noting only that the bed is made. Now she goes downstairs to Lucille.

"I found the trouble," she sings out.

"Did you?" asks Lucille with interest. "Did we have pie or something I forgot about?"

"The trouble is in your own room. Your room feels exactly like a cluttered park after a Fourth of July picnic."

Lucille frowns. "I just simply don't even want to go up there. I wish I could sleep somewhere else."

"Let's make a list," says Mother as they go upstairs. Together they list every possible task. "We'll set the alarm for the end of the hour and see what has happened by then."

When the alarm rings, the room is straight even to the dresser drawers. But Lucille has not finished. She has decided to sew on three buttons, to take her red dress to the cleaners, to catch up on her diary. Seldom has a more cheerful Lucille gone off to bed at eight simply radiating good nature and achievement.

In this case, the answer to Lucille's problem lay in helping her to understand that unhappy states of mind may very logically be the result of her own actions, or of procrastination or laziness or subterfuge or almost anything which produces a sense of guilt.

Children question their relationship to laws and customs, even more demandingly than their relationship to the things with which they must deal. They seem forever weighing observations and drawing conclusions about the rules made by adults. Sometimes the process comes to the surface where a parent may observe it. For instance, Benny is a country cousin, aged eight, on his first visit to his city cousin Alfred, aged nine. Both are walking down the street with their mothers when an argument comes up over the red and green lights at the intersections.

"Who said we have to wait for a green light?" asks Benny.

"The law said so," Alfred answers quickly. "This city's full of law."

By this time they have crossed the street but Benny is walking backwards in order to watch the changing lights. "What's the law?" asks Benny.

"Yes, what is the law, Alfred?" asks his mother.

"It's what the policemen decide they'll arrest you for if you don't do," explains Alfred.

"The policemen don't decide on the laws," says his mother. "They only carry out the law. They do what the law tells them to do — arrest people who speed or drive against the lights or break into houses and things like that."

"Then who makes the laws to begin with?"

"Different laws are made by different groups," says his mother, beginning to feel a little vague herself. "Traffic laws are made by the City Council."

"What's the City Council?"

"The City Council is a group of men who govern the city. They get together and decide what regulations will be best for all these thousands of people who live here. If each person had to make up his own mind when to cross the street, there would be many more accidents. On some streets the cars would tear along all day and the people who are waiting to cross might never have a chance. So the City Council decides the traffic regulations and then lets everybody know about them."

"Do they write everybody a letter?" asks Benny.

"They publish new regulations in the newspapers. Sometimes they also post placards so that people walking along will stop to read the notices."

"They have another way," cries Alfred in sudden excitement. "My father showed me. When you get your automobile license, they send you a little book with all the rules in it."

"But what if you don't get a book and you don't read the newspapers and you didn't see the signs? Then you can drive the way you want to," announces argumentative Benny.

"Oh no, young man," says his own mother. " 'Ignorance of the law is no excuse.' When a law is made, it is usually published in newspapers as your aunt said, and copies are sent to the lawyers and honest efforts are made to let people know about it. But it begins to operate no matter whether people have heard of it or not."

"That isn't fair," says Benny. "I wouldn't go to jail for breaking a law I never heard about."

The children having reached the park, law gives way

to a war whoop. But evidently the discussion remains in the boy's mind because that night Benny says to his father, "You have to go to jail for things you never heard about. Do you call that fair?"

Now Benny may be only eight but he has articulated a thought which affects the inner climate of almost every child's mind every day, and many children's minds all the time. Is it fair? If Benny's father can point up the reasonableness of the law governing traffic lights so that Benny understands how the safety of all is protected by the cooperation of all, and the necessity of maintaining law even in the face of possible ignorance of its very existence, then he really has given his son a major insight.

Understanding is the bridge between the outer and the inner worlds. A child needs to know *how* nature performs, including human nature, and then *why*, and finally what he is supposed to do about it. A parent who can help him arrive at these insights in regard to specific incidents, demands, and persons makes it possible for him to learn to generalize and deduce, so that gradually he can deal with his environment, adjust to his fellows, and become his mature self. A terrific amount of conformity is required of the young and the keynote of co-operation is probably fairness. Most children have a keen sense of justice; even very young children respond affirmatively to the need for fair play. And when a course of action seems fair, a child's emotions are likely to be expansive, even when he must do something he may prefer not to do.

On the other hand, when a child concludes he is being unfairly put upon by his parents or teachers, by his peers, or even by "the law," then resentment festers and his mind is likely to turn to thoughts of reprisal. He maneuvers his inner resources into position for attacking the outer world of circumstance. Or else he withdraws from the unfair conditions over which he has no control and lives entirely in a world he can manipulate to his liking. If his resentment against unfairness leads him to action which displeases those more powerful than he, he may find himself subject to punishment or threat, or — worse — to withdrawal of approval. Then he is indeed insecure — for who is he apart from those with whom he has constant commerce? Feeling alone, unloved, and nobody, he develops a gnawing unreasoned fear. Either he will make almost any concession to bring about acceptance, or he will retreat still further from the "real" world of outer demands. Most children never reach extremes in either direction, but they flounder and waste energy that might be spent in achieving full growth as personalities.

Is it any wonder, then, that their questions are important? And especially the questions they do not ask. Here we are, mere parents, responsible for the next generation upon whose wisdom and serenity of judgment the future of the world depends! No respite from parenthood. Our best hope appears in keeping pliable, teachable, and invincibly loving.

IV. What of God?

A fire-mist and a planet,
A crystal and a cell,
A jelly fish and a saurian,
And caves where the cave men dwell;
Then a sense of law and beauty,
And a face turned from the clod—
Some call it Evolution,
And others call it God.

WILLIAM CARRUTH (*Each in His Own Tongue*)

An editor of one of the national magazines for parents remarks that she receives more letters about the child and religion than about any other concern of parents for their children. Also that she finds these questions the most difficult to answer, either by personal reply or by article. In other sorts of problems — education, sex, food, play — parents across the land have enough common experience and enough common vacabulary so that a writer can speak to a great many persons at the same time. But in matters of religion, says the editor, neighbors who live next door to each other and apparently carry on a common social and business life, may be decades, if not centuries, apart.

At first glance it seems strange that religion, which deals with the meaning of life, should signify such different things to different people. The materials of living are more or less the same for all of us. Why then should we interpret them so differently? But after all, no matter how individual experience appears to conform to a general pattern,

57

it *is* different for each person. Life is one thing to the well fed, another to the hungry.] The emotions of the successful hunter are not the emotions of one who has to watch the chase from afar. Back when the world began or now, what could the hunter say about life to one who must sit apart? Or the contemplator to the hunter? And yet each, having found certain meanings, is inclined to decree, "This is *the* meaning and therefore you must do thus and so."

[Fundamentally the meaning we extract from life is our religion. In some way we all deal with first causes and final ends, with time values, with personality relationships. We either affirm or deny a Supreme Being. These concerns are the domain of religion. But not of religion exclusively; they may be also matters of psychological, sociological, or philosophical interest. These concerns, reduced to simplicites, are also the domain of the child whose growing up entails finding his place in the universe. Hence a child is bound to ask religious questions. But here again his religious questions are not exclusively religious. In his mind they do not fall into categories; he is just asking about life.]

If a child's question about his beginning includes use of the term "God," our adult mind is likely to trigger a response, "Now I must give him a sound religious answer," and so we are apt to miss the core of the question in our endeavor to pass on our own God-meaning. For questions we feel to be religious we get our religious terminology down off a high shelf of memory and dust off the precious phrases quickly in order to hand them over to our children. Then stand amazed that they view them as curios.

This whole matter of religious terminology is important because theological terms have less currency in the life of a child of grade-school age than was the case two generations ago; if we are going to use them to answer questions then we have to make them clear, to bring them into the child's experience.

Horace, aged twelve, has grown up in a minister's family in which the concerns of religion are discussed casually and naturally. One Sunday he goes with a friend to Sunday School in a Jewish Reformed temple, where the boys of his grade are studying the great Jewish reformers, including Jesus. In the course of the lesson, the Jewish teacher explains a bit of the Christian theology which has developed from the teachings of Jesus. In great amazement, Horace comes home and calls to his mother: "Mother, where are you? Listen, Mother, did you ever hear about the Three in One?"

"Did I ever hear of what? Come up here," says Mother.

Horace bounds upstairs. "Did you ever hear about the Three in One — Father, Son and Holy Ghost, blessed Trinity in one Godhead?"

"Why, Horace," remonstrates mother, "you've heard of the Trinity all of your life."

"Not until this morning. Mr. Levy told the boys — " And then Horace repeats the traditional Christian tenets of which, until that morning, he had been completely unaware.

Horace's mother's responsibility is to reply in words which have current meaning for the boy, whether she chooses to go into the matter of the unique divinity of Jesus as the son of God and his unique relationship to the Holy Ghost, or chooses to outline the historical development of the terms, or frankly to say that the concept of the Trinity seems rather meaningless to her.

Whatever she says, Horace's mother has become a theologian — the last thing, probably, she ever dreamed of becoming — because in derivation the word "theology" means "to speak of God." A parent has not only to speak of God but actually to have some systematic ideas about God, his creation and its purpose. So here we are, mere parents, amateurs and novices, in a highly precarious position because as soon as we begin to speak *about* God we are likely to sound to our children as if we were speaking *for* God. We say the final word. Nor is parental theological dogmatism confined to the Christian point of view, for the no-god idea may also be presented as an absolute, promulgated with the authority of a high priest. All too-sure people are dangerous, especially parents.

"Mother, do you believe in God?" "Daddy, you do think there's a God some place, don't you?" In some form every child asks these questions. And essentially there are only three answers. The first answer is, "Yes, of course." The second is, "No." The third is, "It depends upon what you mean by God."

Parents who answer, "Yes, of course," are likely to be asked for proof. "How do you know?" is a favorite demand of the young. Some parents will then turn to the Bible. "Here is his holy word. Here is the story of his revelation of himself. Here is the history of his dealings with men since time began." And for some children, the Bible record is proof enough, especially when it seems sufficient to their parents. But many children will argue on, unsatisfied with proof from the Scriptures. "It seems to me that some people just wrote down what they thought about God in a book we call the Bible, but that doesn't prove there is a God. They might be completely mistaken. And even if there is some kind of God, he may not be at all as the Bible pictures him. Who is going to say what God is like?"

"The church." This answer is sufficient for many parents and they pass it on as sufficient for their children. In each generation the church has had ecclesiastical authorities whose business it is to make the final ruling as to what the Scriptures mean and what the term "God" shall signify. These specialists are set apart for their task just as specialists in medicine or law or architecture become authorities by dint of their studies and experience. Among the most successful parents of our generation, as of other generations, are some who are proud and glad to accord the final authority to these specialists. They are relieved that the individual need not carry all the responsibility for figuring out his own idea of God and his relationship to God. He has access to the wisdom of the priest. All orthodox Roman Catholics allow the church to make the final answer to questions about God's nature and being.

But to the question, "Is there a God?" some parents who answer quickly and unequivocally, "Of course there is a God," do not cite the authority of the Scriptures or of the church to prove their point. They rely upon what they feel to be their own experience.

"How do you know there is a God, Daddy?" asks Pamela, who dearly likes to propound large questions when she and her father have finished their game of chess by the fire. She realizes that her father tempers his answers, as he does his game, to her ten-year-old capacity but just the same both game and discussion make her feel very grown up. This question has come up because a boy in the fifth grade spoke right out in class when they were learning the Gettysburg Address and said "this nation under God" didn't make sense because he didn't believe in God.

Her father tips back in his chair, hands behind his head, and smiles. But he speaks gravely. "How do I know there is a God? I'm always aware of his presence; that's how I know."

"You mean like when we go out at night and learn a new constellation." On a starry night Pamela has often heard her father quote, "The heavens declare the glory of God"; sometimes right to the end of the Psalm.

"I mean that but more. I mean that when I turn to God for help, I get an answer." Her father speaks with decision, the way he always speaks about something he knows.

"You mean when we pray," Pamela agrees. She can't remember when she first began to pray.

"I mean that, too, but more. I mean I'm always aware of a Presence with me — Someone tender but stern and demanding, Someone who expects me to be more than I now am and shows me the way moment by moment."

"I guess I know," Pamela agrees. "It's like that with me, too, but it's kind of a hard thing to tell a person who doesn't already know."

Disclosure of experience of God *is* difficult to impart if, as Pamela points out, one starts cold with a person who has no experience of his own. But parents who experience God's presence cannot help imparting the fact to their children while the children are still so small that they never remember when they first learned how their parents feel about God. Questions grow along with children; answers grow as parents grow. Occasionally a discussion stands out, but the constant exchange of experience builds the total answer. The sort of parent who attests his faith in God by his experience may or may not identify himself with the church and the teaching of the Bible. He may be a Christian or he may be a Taoist; he may bear the name of any one of a number of "religions" or of no system at all. He may feel no need of assembling himself with other people for common worship, no need of mediating priests or instructing parsons. There is no gainsaying the fact that the human spirit finds its sufficiency in a variety of experiences, perhaps all of them tapping at the same source. The most that a parent can do for a child, even when he answers the question of God with an unequivocal "yes," is to affirm that he himself is fed by certain deep springs and to disclose his way of reaching them.

The second kind of answer to the question "Is there a God?" may be a definite negative.

"Of course there is no God. 'God' is an outgrown idea which man invented before he had figured out the laws of nature. The savage, for instance, could not understand the laws of rain and its capricious habits, so he laid the fact that it did not always come when needed to the whim or anger of some superior being who had moods like his own. He did not understand the laws of health so he thought that someone outside his ken sent disease by way of punishment. He called this someone 'God.' He did not understand the nature of fire, the power of the sea, the habits of the sun and moon and stars. So he predicated some personality behind the universe making it work as it did work. He called this personality 'God.'"

Perhaps the child thinks over the answer for a while and then ventures, "But there are still a lot of things we do not understand. Maybe they are the things which only God can understand, and that's one reason people believe there is a God because there couldn't be an operating universe unless some kind of a super-Somebody understood what was going on."

To which the parent replies, "There are plenty of phenomena we don't understand. It may take thousands of years to learn all we need to know about the universe. But we already know that all life develops according to law. Our concern is to find out these laws. The burden falls on us to live in harmony with the laws of the universe rather than to predicate some God to account for them and expect him to adjust the laws to our liking."

The conclusive "no" answer which maintains that reality

is a machine expressing an unself-conscious amoral law,
and the explicit "yes" answer which can attest the very
nature of God and delineate his attributes, may have the
same difficulty of failing to persuade by too great assurance.

There is a third group of parents who answer the question about God with the phrase, "It depends upon what
you mean by God." Perhaps they know less than the first
two groups. Perhaps they know more. Or perhaps they
are fearful of any final word. They leave open a few
windows for free winds of doubt.

Roscoe is a sturdy thirteen-year-old, seldom preoccupied
by speculative interest, usually absorbed in his many activities. His father is a physician who does research on cancer.
He is not a churchman and has never discussed religion in
any way with his children. Roscoe has been to church two
or three times in his life when he trailed along with playmates who went habitually.

One day Roscoe comes into the house, finds his father
in the living room alone, and propounds a sudden question.
"Pop, do you believe in God?"

His father puts down the book he is reading. "It depends," he answers, "on what you mean by God."

"I just mean — God," says Roscoe with an indefinite
gesture. "You know, the God that made the world and
made people and . . ." his sentence trails off.

"Personally I don't use the word 'God,' son. I think
there are better words for what we mean. I don't think
that anyone 'made' the world. It came into being out of
some vast chaos whose original form we do not yet understand. Somehow this whirling ball we call the earth shot
off into space and found an orbit of its own. As its crust
cooled, there finally emerged water and land, the oceans
and the continents. Cells of living matter took on form.
No one can positively say how living matter began —

yet. We can only stake out a borderland in which organic and inorganic matter meet." He looks at Roscoe's eager face, straining to take in what he means. "Organic and inorganic matter — that means everything living or, as we say, dead, as stones are dead."

Roscoe nods, real comprehension in his eyes.

"The whole concept of matter has changed in my generation. Some of our best scientists remind us that the study of small-scale phenomena has taken every vestige of corporeality from matter and resolved the material universe into radiations and waves, into atoms, protons, and electrons." He looks at Roscoe and tries again. "What I mean is, that basically matter is energy, see? It isn't solid as we used to think; it pulses the way light does — somewhat. There is no substantiality to what we used to call matter."

Roscoe nods again. "I know about atoms, and about splitting them apart, and I know about released energy."

"Furthermore," his father goes on, warming to his subject in the presence of so eager an audience, "there isn't any proof but that these waves and radiations may be akin to the stuff that thoughts are made of. And if thoughts, perhaps a consciousness, and if consciousness, perhaps purpose. But metrical conceptions and mathematical symbols give us no information as to what the purpose of life may be."

Roscoe is still hanging on.

"What I mean is, we don't know the source and we don't know the purpose of life. So to generalize a source we do not apprehend under the term 'God,' and to set him up as a superior sort of being, seems to me a vague abstraction."

"You mean — we can get along without God?" There is some amazement in Roscoe's voice.

"Not exactly," his father replies. "I mean that we needn't be so concerned as to what he is like, exactly. The important thing is to find out the nature of the universe. That is something we can go to work on. And the knowledge we gain can be used for the good of mankind."

Roscoe thinks for a moment, then looks into the face of his parent who has really been trying to share his best insight. "Well, if you did believe it was God that was behind all of those things, then you'd have to go to church to worship him, wouldn't you?"

"Some people feel they have to go to church to worship. But it seems to me that one's respect for the purposes of nature is intrinsic."

Roscoe's eyes brighten. "You mean you feel — respectful about the way everything outdoors and in the sea and under miscroscopes seems to work out."

"I mean in any sort of science, say chemistry or biology, the laws are so intricate and dependable that they draw forth awe and wonder. When a man works with a constant wonder he doesn't need a special time and place — such as church at eleven on Sunday mornings — to express the profound humility with which he approaches his task of finding out more about life. When he accomplishes something, he does not need to gather his friends together to sing hymns of praise. His relationship to his work is a sort of steady compact with life. If he gets too proud over what he has done and rests back on his laurels, then nature just doesn't open any more secrets to him. But if he keeps on working, then life gives him more understanding to work with. I think the attitude of continual respect for life is more important than what you call 'worship.' "

Roscoe, hunched in a big chair, is obviously thinking over what his father has said. But he frowns, because his father's point of view seems to lay a terrific burden on people.

His father senses something of what is in his mind and remarks, "We aren't after the easier thing. We're after the truth if we can find it."

Roscoe nods slowly. His father's whole life backs up what he has just said. He slides out of his chair, still thinking, and starts back to play. Then he stops in the doorway. "When I grow up I'm going into research, too. I'll operate on everybody and find out everything." A minute later the kitchen door bangs. Roscoe is through with his theological considerations for this day.

But he will come back some time. It may be years later but he will come back inevitably to ask: "In an impersonal world, how much do I matter? If I do 'right' or 'wrong' how much ultimate difference does it make? Without a God to hold me to accounting, it's pretty much my own choice whether I'm a waster or a builder."

And then his father will have to answer: "Yes, it is up to you and to your fellows. You have high expectations for yourself and if you choose to suffer the defeat of not living up to them, then that's your own hell. And it's enough. If you run amuck of the customs society has declared to be good and useful, then society will make you pay one way or another. But that's small punishment beside the gnawing defeat of having let yourself down."

"And where do I get the power to hold myself up?" cries this older Roscoe to his father.

"The power comes with the high expectations. You generate it as you go. You build a reserve of power through your habits of accomplishment. Nature never cheats. She'll play your game and sustain your efforts as long as you demand it of her."

Now this older Roscoe may push on to find that the

power which sustains him appears too personal for an abstraction. He may experience its compassion, its cleansing, its upholding, its quickening, its love. And if he ultimately addresses it as *Father*, the term derives its warmth and integrity from his experience with his human parent.

There is still another way of saying, "It depends upon what you mean by God."

Jane's father is a physicist and Jane, now fifteen and already a senior in high school, firmly expects to follow in his field. She thinks beyond her years, and today she is reporting a recent examination on the subject of matter.

"I tell you, Dad, when matter is defined as energy, it seems to me the term *God* is pretty well ruled out." She looks at her father sideways, wondering how he will take her latest adult conclusion. "Energy in its various forms accounts for every force in this universe."

"Only in a sense," her father answers, his serious tone paying her all the respect he would pay a colleague. "It's only partially true that energy is all. Take a living organism. Broken into its chemical constituents, it is energy, but each cell is energy in an organized pattern. Each cell is not just an aggregate but an architecture. In any organism the vital functions of growth, reproduction, and adaptation can be studied in isolation, but they can't be understood outside the dynamic whole, their sum. There is an underlying pattern of protoplasmic control. Where does that pattern originate?"

"I know what you're trying to make me say," Jane grins. "You're at the old dodge of telling me that a pattern presupposes a pattern-maker."

Her father smiles back, wrinkling his big forehead. "At least I'm going to say that a pattern presupposes an end in view. The philosophers call it teleology, the idea of purpose. Every living cell, and every organ composed of cells, appears to have a purpose. And it looks to me as if the psychosomatic organization known as man also has a purpose.

"It's plain enough that the body has a purpose," Jane agrees. "It has to reproduce its kind."

Her father nods. "It's relatively easy to predicate a purpose for the somatic part of the combination: bodies mature and reproduce; they also adapt and develop in an evolutionary way. But here's an interesting thing: they don't develop independent of the psyche."

"Psyche meaning what?" Jane asks, in a tone which implies, "Now I've got you."

"Meaning individuality — mind-plus — and what that plus is we are not yet sure but we have intimations. Some call it the soul. Something appears to hold the mind and body in partnership, and that something appears to continue in partnership with the mind regardless of the body. I'm going to say that mind-plus seems to have an end in view also, an evolutionary end, and that end appears to be the expansion of consciousness. I'm also going to say that the ultimate expansion of consciousness may disclose the whole pattern of the universe. And that in seeing it we may become one with it, submerging our individuated selves without losing our identity. And I'm going to say that behind and throughout the whole, there is God." Her father draws the car to a stop at the crest of the hill as he often does.

Jane looks over the expanse of countryside. Then she turns to her father. "And I'm going to say that's too impersonal for me. If I had a God he'd have to be a personality. He'd have to have a loving, caring mind and heart, just the way old-fashioned people think of him, or there isn't any use in calling him God. And you see, you've just talked that kind of God out of existence."

Her father taps the wheel in a little tune of his own. "Never. Consciousness at its widest is personality at its biggest. The mind behind the universe, being consciousness at its acme, is compassion as well as law. Infinite compassion. Love, if you will. That kind of consciousness is the quickening principle which not only brings life into being but patterns it after Itself. Himself is a better word because we can't think of love as impersonal, however far above self-involvement it may be. For me that encompassing heart of the universe — too large to be confined in space or time but pervasive enough to attend our least yearning — that's God."

For a moment Jane makes no reply. Then she says, "You're sweet, Dad. I know you know more than I do, but still I just can't take in such a big God."

Her father starts up the car. "You couldn't do with a lesser God."

Jane doesn't say anything for a while and then she turns a happy face to her father. "It's lovely, isn't it, to feel ourselves getting bigger ideas all the time." Whereupon she looks apologetic, almost embarrassed. "I mean there are so many kinds of curiosity and it's kind of nice when your curiosity sort of seems to get some place. That's why I want to be a physicist."

"You never need to apologize for curiosity whether it appears to get some place or not. It's the purest of the passions, Jane. Understanding just for the love of it is about as swell an experience as comes man's way."

They ride in silence for a while. Jane is in a state of alert passivity from which insight rises. Her father knows when not to intrude with words. Of course he knows that in their talk they haven't proved anything about God, one way or the other, but he feels that Jane won't discard the idea of God too quickly. She has something to grow up to.

Another kind of parent might have spoken more simply. "I know here is a God because when I turn with a need beyond human help, I find my need answered. The One-who-answers I call God. He gives me wisdom and more courage than I ever dreamed of having. He even gives me joy in the midst of hardship; joy because I know he is available. This is a thing I've found through experience, the way we learn all other things we're sure of. I know there is a God and you can depend on it."

Now this kind of parent is not talking generalities, as the inexperienced might conclude. He is communicating experience at a deep level. For him that experience is incontrovertible.

Among those who accept the idea of God, it is one thing merely to accept an intellectual concept and it is quite another to go to work ordering one's days on the basis of that idea. In a practical sense, adults probably accept only as much of an idea of God as they can put to work in their daily lives. Certainly a child either "uses" his God or ignores him. The child's ideas and his actions are all of one piece. Sometimes an idea may push ahead of action; sometimes action appears to outreach the original concept, which merely means that the concept is enlarged as it is experienced. A child's experience of God, as of anything else, is expressed in his play as readily as in any of his real-life relationships.

Stuart was five the summer he went to the north Wisconsin woods to live on a lake. Day after day he accompanied his mother to an old farm at the head of the lake where milk and vegetables were sold. For the children, the farm was important because of the large crop of kittens, all "wild," living on the edge of the woods and refusing to come at any human's call. Through many years on that farm, mother cats had raised kittens who grew up and

raised more kittens, most of them the color of burnished
gold. In and out of the farm buildings, the plump cats
and kittens played hide-and-seek. But only occasionally
could one be coaxed within a few yards of the onlooker.
On various occasions Stuart had tried to play with the
family of kittens who lived under the ice house. The
roundest, coyest one of all he named "Fireball." Fireball
got so she would go into an ecstasy of excitement over a
moving string of grapevine and follow the boy all around
the yard. But Fireball would not be caught. The farm
lady had said that if Stuart could catch her he certainly
might have her to take home.

One afternoon Stuart had a long time to wait at the farm,
so he played with the kittens. Fireball, tired out with play
— or as nearly tired out as a kitten will admit — finally
crept right up to the spot where Stuart lay on the grass —
as nearly tired out as a boy will admit — and curled herself
into a ball against his chest. There she purred most heartily. Mother from the porch saw the kitten and called
the farm lady who called the cook who called the hands.
Everyone surveyed the spectacle of the wild kitten curled
in the arms of a small human.

At last it was time for Stuart to leave. He started down
to the boat landing with the kitten jumping a his heels
like a puppy. Onto the dock walked Stuart and onto the
dock walked Fireball. The boy leaned over to give the
kitten a last pat. She snuggled against his bare legs and
scratched clawlessly at his ankles. Reluctantly Stuart
picked her up and set her back on land, ran down the
dock and hopped into the boat. The kitten leaped to the
end of the dock where she stood mewing lustily, watched
by the entire farm family on the porch and by the other
cats peering out from beneath the ice house. The boat
pulled way. And then, when the boat was some six or

eight feet from the dock, the kitten jumped into the lake and swam for the boat. Back-paddling quickly, mother met the kitten halfway and Stuart leaned over the side of the boat to lift in a very wet bit of kitten.

Rolling the kitten into his sweater, Stuart turned to his mother with wide eyes. "Fireball thinks I'm God." And then to the kitten, "There, there, you don't need to shiver. God's got you all safe and warm."

The child continued in the role of God without comment from any member of the family. Each morning as soon as the fire was started in the kitchen stove, he heated the kitten's milk, poured it into her saucer and took it to her corner. "God's feeding you," he would say. Or if the family were going away for any afternoon, he would pick up the kitten and carry her from her basket to her sandbox to her saucer of milk, and back to her basket, making sure she knew where everything was and then, giving her a final pat, he would add, "You think God's gone away but God will remember about you all the time and you'll be all right."

Evidently he had spun the theory that for all practical kitten purposes safety consisted in existing "in the mind of God," as the earlier theologians might have said.

One day a great-aunt came to visit and overheard Stuart's remark to the kitten, "God won't let Ben's dog come near you."

"Goodness me," she said in genuine concern, "it's pure sacrilege to let a child talk as if he were God Almighty."

"He'll probably never come nearer to God than when he's trying to act like him," said father calmly.

The idea of being God to the small cat wore off, as children's ideas do wear off. Stuart went away for two weeks. When he returned home he was still just as fond of the cat but he never again referred to himself as God —

until one day when he was twelve years old. Walking along a country road one evening with his father, he said "Once when I was quite young I had a kitten named Fireball. Do you remember?"

"I remember. She was about the cutest kitten we ever had."

"Wasn't she! Well, sir, I thought that the cat thought I was God so I used to try to act like God when I was alone. Evenings like this, I pretended I walked on the clouds and whenever I came to poor children's houses I dropped blessings on them. It seemed awfully lonesome for children to live the year round way out here in tar-paper houses and hardly ever have any company. I pretended I was God riding along the old roads with a wagonload of surprise packages and leaving one in every mailbox. I still think of that every time I go by country mailboxes and some day I'm going to do it."

"While you're at it, you might leave a little more livestock for the barns and a few washing machines for the women."

Stuart walked on without comment for a bit and then remarked: "I guess there are some things even God can't do without help. He can't make washing machines rain from heaven. And he can't make dairy cows walk down out of clouds. People have to help themselves."

"It's uphill work sometimes."

"I remember when Fireball thought I was God. I mean when I thought Fireball thought I was God. I remember telling her over and over, 'Even God can't teach you to use a sandbox unless you put your mind to it.'"

Father chuckled to himself, realizing how easily in a child's mind divinity concerns itself with practical affairs, realizing also how lightly and naturally a child may skirt the truths to which wise ones give a lifetime of searching. He spoke to that point. He spoke man to man.

"When you said there are some things even God can't do alone, you were saying one of the most important things about God, at least so it seems to me. He never transgresses human personality. He doesn't 'make' us do a thing. He doesn't even compel us to be good. If he did, he would be only a driving, arbitrary force in a world of automatons. There would be no choices for human beings to make, no struggle to know which things are good to do and which work harm. There would be no passionate devotion to finding out the secrets of nature, no sharpening of man's wits against the universe, no growth. It takes a really great God to leave man free to make his own mistakes."

The boy again walked along for a few moments without speaking. Just as he lengthened his stride to keep step with his father when they walked together, so he seemed to be lengthening his thoughts. "Well, sir, I'll tell you what I think. I think that maybe he doesn't make us do things, just like you say, but I think he wants us to do the right thing so much that you feel him tugging at you."

"You feel his love," suggested father.

"Maybe. You feel he cares so much about you that you can't let him down and so you sort of stop and wait awhile like you were listening and pretty soon you don't feel like doing the shady thing that maybe you were going to do. It just doesn't fit and you don't want to do it any more. And you feel like you'd had a sort of little visit although you didn't say anything. I mean you didn't pray or anything, and of course he didn't really say anything either." Stuart paused. "At least that's how we talk things over."

"We." Father found his throat tightening. How naturally the boy said it. And here he had been wondering lately if his noisy young son, banging off to play with three whoops and a holler, ever had a serious thought.

One thing Stuart's father did not consciously realize, although any thoughtful neighbor could have told him. His son had been feeling the compelling love of God partly because he felt also the compelling love of his father whose quick understanding and high integrity were always behind the boy like a bulwark. Any child's experience of God is rather likely to be set in the mold of his experience with earthly parenthood.

But the child's idea of God is not always expressed overtly, so that his parent can say, "Look, he is playing God." Sometimes, to be sure, a child may stand on a chair throwing real or imaginary balls into the air as he creates a universe and tosses the stars into space. Or the fancy of another child may be caught by the story of the ark and, not content to be Noah, he is Jehovah the Lord warning the wicked, calling on Noah to prepare the ark, finally rounding up the animals two by two so that Noah can coax them to safety. God the creator seems to appeal to the small child, especially to the child who asks insistent questions about the beginnings of things: Who made me? How was the first man made? How was the world made? Who did it? Then who made God?

This sort of child, asking how-questions, is likely to relive the beginnings of all sorts of things in his play, although he may not go through the physical motions of making things. He may sit ever so still, a concentrated bundle of imagination, playing all the stories in his mind. Unlike the child who acts out his creations, he may not be aware that he is playing God. He is merely off on the edge of somewhere, stretching his mind to take in the ideas of time and space and an ultimate beginning. If he lives in a household which uses the term "God," he is unconsciously giving the word content for himself. He is letting his own emotions inflate the ideas which have come from his parents until, like a handful of tugging balloons, they almost pull him off his feet.

One way or another, the dominant characteristics of a child's God will almost always reveal themselves in his play. Even when he does not think of himself as pretending he is God, still he orders events on a large scale, giving himself tremendous power of the sort he would credit to God if his ideas were forced into words. Jack with his toy soldiers goes forth to fight the enemy, right and might on his side, daring storm and flood as well as bullets. Ellen, scarcely six, plays orphans' asylum with number cards, letting the numbers stand for the ages of the children and gathering each child with its own particular story of hardship into the affection and responsibilities of the orphans' home. Day after day she plays the game, never seeming to tire of inventing new children.

Jack and Ellen are in the same Sunday school class. When a chance question about God sets all the children to answering at once, Jack says: "God punishes those that don't do right. He lets the good armies blow them to pieces. He makes earthquakes and shakes them up. He can do anything he wants to. No matter where they run to, he can always catch them in the end." Ellen says: "God finds out about everybody that's having a hard time, like children who don't have parents and people in hospitals and the poor and newsboys. Pretty soon he thinks up a way to help them get more to eat and have a birthday party and things."

Jack and Ellen listen to each other's answers, each ready to fly to the protection of his own God but also uneasily aware that perhaps there is something in the other's idea.

A week later, chance and a May morning make neighbors of the two children. They begin to play together. They play soldier and they play orphans. One play modifies the other until, quite unconsciously, of course, both children are also "playing God" from much the same point of view.

As in other matters, a parent most persuasively passes on to his child his own convinced point of view. There is small use in a father's extolling the wonders of drinking milk if he wrinkles his own nose at the very thought. Likewise there is small effect in a mother's counseling a child to turn to God with his troubles if she runs to the neighbors, and the fortuneteller with her own anxieties. When adult actions and words fly off at different tangents, children are not on a hearing level. On the other hand, when parents have an experience of God it is difficult to keep the fact out of the conversation.

Nothing persuades like a demonstration. A mother who knows she is ruffled, angry, sharp-spoken and so goes to her room to ask God's help, then returns to the family *melee* gentled, even humorous, scarcely needs to mention that she has had an experience of God's restorative presence. She acts out her understanding of God as surely as ever a child plays God. Her experience becomes her medium of exchange with her own edgy child. Our theory of reality, including God, makes its mark on us and all our ways, and we "make" our child in the imagine of our God.

V. What of Jesus?

But Thee, but Thee, O sovereign Seer of time,
But Thee, O poets' Poet, Wisdom's Tongue,
But Thee, O man's best Man, O love's best Love,
O perfect life in perfect labor writ,
O all men's Comrade, Servant, King, or Priest,...

SIDNEY LANIER (*The Crystal*)

Was Jesus a real man who truly lived or did someone just make him up like King Arthur? How can you prove he really lived? Do you believe that Jesus never had any father except God? Do you believe that he performed miracles like changing water into wine, and feeding five thousand people with those tiny loaves and fishes, and walking on the water? And if he did perform miracles, what help is that to us?

If Jesus was so good, why did God make him suffer on a cross and die? But if he was divine, how could he feel any pain? Did he truly rise from the dead? Do you believe that Jesus really meant to start a church? Doesn't it make him sound awfully conceited to be going around telling people to worship him? Or did someone else think up the idea of worshiping him after he was dead?

Anyhow, why should Jesus matter so much to *us*? What do *you* think of him?

Probably three observations can safely be made about the answers that parents will make to these customary questions of their children. First, there is a group of parents who can answer wholeheartedly within the framework of traditional Christian theology. Their children's questions never catch them unprepared because at all times they know exactly what they believe.

Jessie Holsman has been what her father fondly designates "a snub-nosed enigma" since she was four and was noticed stopping stock-still in the middle of a game of tag because she had suddenly "thought a poem." Ever since, her young life to the age of twelve has been a combination of outdoor games, at which she excels, and rapt reading and inventing of poetry. One day she comes to her mother and asks, "What do people mean when they say, 'Do you believe in Jesus?'"

Her mother puts down the sock she is darning and looks at her daughter earnestly for a moment while she hunts for words. "People mean different things, I think. But usually the question means, Do you believe that Jesus was the son of God and that he suffered for our sins and died for us, that he was raised from the dead and ascended to heaven, that he will come again some day to judge the living and the dead, and that all who believe in him will have everlasting life?"

"My, that's a lot," says Jessie thoughtfully. "Do you believe all that?" She looks directly into her mother's eyes.

Her mother looks back at her, confidently. "Yes, I do believe all that."

"But I don't exactly understand it all," says Jessie.

"Neither do I," her mother acknowledges, "but I believe it. The story as I read it in the Bible is so simple and direct that I see no reason to doubt it. And the beliefs which the church has long held about Jesus seem to me reasonable and secure. So I believe in him even when I don't understand exactly how he could have ascended into heaven or how he will come again."

Jessie starts out of the room slowly as if the conversation

were finished, gets as far as the dining-room door and turns back. "Well, but mother, what difference does it make if you do believe in Jesus? Maybe you may get everlasting life, but what difference does believing in him make now?"

"It makes a difference in the way I act. It makes a difference every day of my life, every hour of the day. I'm always thinking to myself, 'Jesus wouldn't make that cross answer I'm about to make. He would hold his peace, or say something helpful.' Or I say to myself, 'Jesus wouldn't sit contentedly at home when people along the river flats live in hovels and have no fires to keep out the cold. He'd be doing something about their needs.'"

"You do something about their needs; you're always gathering up clothes for them and all sorts of things."

"I try to do things, but the reason I do them is because I know Jesus would want me to." Her mother speaks simply and surely.

"Does he really matter that much to you, Mother?"

"He matters much more than that. When I walk in the woods on Grandfather's farm, I think to myself, God made a beautiful world for his children but it's Jesus who puts meaning into it all because he showed us the love of God. He loved us so much that he could give up his life for us."

"I'll tell you, Mother, he doesn't mean that much to me. But I'm going to get him to." The shy, earnest look in her eyes says, "I want to be like you, Mother, and if he's the one who makes you the way you are, then I want to know him the way you do."

Jessie starts from the room again, humming happily. She realizes that she doesn't understand everything her mother has said but she feels secure and at the same time rather heroic. She hopes she will have a very hard life full of sacrifices because she feels that she not only wants to do something worthy of this one who died for her but that somehow he will give her the strength to do it. That night she writes a little poem which begins,

> I know not why I trust him so
> Except he trusted me.

An older Jessie might have pressed the theological implications of some of her mother's statements. "Was Jesus the son of God in a different way than we are children of God?"

"Yes, indeed. God gave him his own miraculous powers so that men would know he was God as well as man. God sent him into the world to make plain by his life what was expected of mankind. And in the world he remained sinless, perfect, as God is perfect."

An adolescent is apt to press on. "But when you say he was sinless, do you mean he could not sin? The Bible account says he was tempted in all points as we are tempted."

"He was tempted, but having God's nature he could not have sinned."

Some children will argue the point of Jesus' dying for the sins of the world. "Why do we call him *our* Savior? How could he die for us when we were not yet born?"

"He died for all who had sin in themselves, as all men have, both those then living and those yet to be born. He took their sins upon himself and offered his life to God in their behalf — the eternal sacrifice."

"Did he know he was the Son of God?"

"He knew. He said, 'The Father and I are one.'"

The extent of a child's theological questions about Jesus depends, of course, upon what theological claims he has heard. A child is not born with an interest in the Trinity or the virgin birth. These are considerations that come to his attention through hearing the talk of his elders, listening to sermons, learning the creed, receiving instructions about church membership. Many parents pass on creedal statements without actually understanding them. There are eternal mysteries, they feel, beyond their ken, and so they pass on to their children a conviction which may outspan reason. Children have considerable capacity to accept, especially as regards mysteries. And great capacity to idealize and idolize a personality which generations have called the Savior of the world. As they strive to follow the teachings of Jesus, and contemplate his flawless life, they are quite willing to acknowledge that this man must have been the very Son of God.

But there is a second and not inconsiderable group of parents who feel that all such theological talk is meaningless. Jesus, if he lived at all, was a man among men, no doubt a wise teacher, probably with many of the attributes of a leader. But there is no more reason to get excited about him than about many other leaders who have left their imprint on their generation. Actually a child is not likely to question parents who hold this point of view because he knows without asking that Jesus is not a great factor in his parents' lives or they would have mentioned the matter themselves at some time.

Third, there are the parents who do not see Jesus as a theological figure, "very God," one with the Father and the Holy Ghost, but feel him to be much more than a great man in his own generation. They acclaim him the greatest of men and the most Godlike.

The Danforths are not a churchgoing household but they might, nevertheless, be called a religious household because of their unusual sensitivity to the creative side of life and because of their unflagging interest in human welfare. One Christmas Eve, Donald, an energetic eighth-grader, comes into the library where his father is surreptitiously wrapping presents.

"It's a funny thing, Dad, but I never really heard the Christmas story until yesterday when Dick Beach read it at our school program. Yesterday I thought, 'Well, goodnight, this is a real story about a real person who once lived just like we live.' It seems queer, doesn't it, that one person should have so much written and said about him for such a long time. I bet he never thought that people would talk about him this way every time Christmas came around."

His father sits down by the desk and settles back. "You can be right sure he didn't think of Christmas, any more than George Washington thought of the cherry tree's becoming a national symbol of honesty. Celebrations and symbols rise after a man has lived significantly and died without being forgotten."

"I bet he never thought people would make a religion about him." Donald sits down and crosses his legs in his most grownup manner. "I bet he was just a plain good man, and a smart one, and he went around being useful. I bet if he'd lived today he'd been a doctor or a labor leader or a teacher or something more useful than a model for church windows like we think of him."

"I think you could call him more than just a plain good man and a smart one," says the father contemplatively. "He must have been unusually discerning when it came to reading human nature and unusually resourceful in putting his finger on human needs. That's what impressed the people he lived among."

"Most likely he was a swell teacher, the kind that always gets to the point and makes you want to do something about it."

"As you say, he must have been a great teacher, or his

illustrations and parables and stories and arguments wouldn't have been so faithfully treasured. But it isn't his teaching which has made him famous, really. It isn't his teaching which matters most."

"But it's the things he said that people today are always talking about. 'Jesus said this' and 'Jesus said that.'"

"What he said is largely important because of what he did. Most of what he taught had been said before by other wise men. His greatness, and his trouble, began when he got into action. He and his disciples picked the ears of corn and ate them on the Sabbath which was supposed to be kept free of work. He went about curing the sick who were supposed to be incurable. Finally he drove the money-changers out of the temple. That was the piece of civic reform that the city fathers couldn't take. That's when they really got busy to find something they could pin on him so that the law could deal with him. It seems to me that it's the combination of insight and action which gave him what we call immortality. Most great men achieve only one of the two."

"I guess he was really — great," says Donald.

"The greatest," his father replies. "The most like God."

And that was the end of the conversation. But the beginning of Donald's personal interest in Jesus.

Actually there is a fourth kind of answer to questions about the unique character of Jesus. Some adolescents feel that the extraordinary abilities of Jesus, his reported miraculous powers, give him such advantage in meeting life's difficulties that he can scarcely serve as a standard-bearer for ordinary human beings. Why worship one who was superhumanly endowed through no effort of his own? Or why try to follow one whose gifts we can never attain? To which some parents point out that the miraculous powers of Jesus — his ability to heal, as the woman with the issue of blood; to read the mind of a questioner, as with the Samaritan woman at the well; to foretell events, such as the betrayal of Judas and his own death, to talk with the dead, as when he conversed with Moses and Elijah on the Mount of Transfiguration — were by-products of his spiritual development, and that his spiritual attainment was very much his own achievement. He could have made wrong choices, but he did not. He could have misused his growing insight and powers, but he did not. And so his character, his essential endowment, the full reach of his mind, was free to manifest at full capacity. Many of the saints, they point out, have a high degree of this same clarity, simplicity, humility. And they develop, in varying degree, these same gifts which in modern terms we call spiritual healing, clairvoyance, precognition, mediumship. The more fully we come to realize our kinship with God, as Jesus realized his kinship, the more surely extraordinary power is bound to manifest through us. Not "miraculous" powers in any esoteric sense, but powers native to the soul, really. Jesus is tremendously significant, then, because he is the exemplar, the demonstration, of a man at full stature, a true son of God.

Most children, familiar with the life of Jesus, ask questions about his death and resurrection. Being devastatingly logical before their minds are cluttered with doubt and dogma, children are likely to see that his resurrection is the heart of the story about Jesus. But how to reconcile it with the conception of death which is the accretion of their culture? How to straddle two contradictory points of view? Parents are put to it to interpret the reports about Jesus in the light of their own understanding of death.

If Alberta came willingly to set the table it was almost a sure sign there was something on the top of her mind which she wished to talk about. Alberta is one of the seven-year-olds who give themselves completely to the interest of the moment. This night being the night before Easter, she was excited about coloring Easter eggs. Her mother expected an effervescence of chatter. Instead, Alberta set the table with no word at all. She moved quickly but she seemed absorbed in some inner contemplation. When everything was ready, she called her brothers, Grant, who was nine, and Jim, who was eleven. Her father was out of town. The candles were lighted, the plates served, and Alberta spoke.

"Do you believe this talk about how Jesus rose from the dead?"

"Alberta!" came automatically from Mother.

"Grandmother believes it," Alberta said with open skepticism. "I asked her today. She believes that Jesus got hung on a cross and then buried in a grave made like a cave with a rock for a door, and then after three days he just sat up and unwrapped the yards of cloth they had buried him in, and got up and walked out of the grave. She believes that he went around for forty days doing good and then he stepped on a cloud and waved good-by to his disciples and went on up to heaven."

The words did not sound like Grandmother's, but the ideas were plainly enough those she shared with much of Christendom. Certainly Alberta had heard the Easter story often enough so that it should not sound like news to her now. But mother realized that children sometimes hear the same thing over and over a great many times before it finally lays hold on the imagination to the point where it must be accepted or rejected. Before she could reply to Alberta, Jim took up the argument.

"Yes, do you believe that story, Mother? Brad says to me today, 'Why do church people make such a fuss about

Easter?' His folks don't go to church and they get along just as good."

" 'Just as well,' " Mother corrected, still sorting her ideas for a convincing answer.

"Just as well. I told Brad that I don't know why we make such a fuss about Easter, except that it's kind of a celebration left over from the days when everybody believed those things and now no one wants to hurt the feelings of those who still believe that way, so everyone keeps on acting as if they still believed that way, too. Now in our family, if you told Grandmother you didn't believe her ideas about Easter, she'd cry a week. She'd think you didn't believe any of her ideas, and most of her ideas are okay."

"Do you believe that Jesus rose from the dead?" The direct question was Grant's. He was given to direct questions, small argument, and simple "yes" or "no" answers. "Either you believe it or you don't believe it. Yes or no."

"It's this way—to me," said Mother. "You remember when Jesus was living, he tried to help his disciples to understand things the way he saw them. He had a good many new ideas. Big ideas. For instance, the idea of doing good to your enemies. It's a pretty breath-taking idea if you never thought of it before."

"Why, it really is, isn't it?" interrupted Alberta, as if it were new to her that very minute.

Mother went on: "To Jesus' disciples, the idea of loving their enemies was entirely new. And that's the way it was with most of Jesus' ideas: they were new and they were amazing. They were hard to take in and very, very hard to act on. But his disciples were big enough men to realize that the ideas were worth trying. And they did try them. While they were trying, they kept very near to Jesus because they needed his explanations, his strength. You know how it is when someone has an idea that you feel you just have to understand. You feel very near to that person."

The children nodded. They were a family bent on finding out things. It was quite easy to understand how disciples would cling to a really good teacher.

Mother continued: "Then all of a sudden, before the disciples ever dreamed that such a thing could happen, along came the enemies of Jesus and worked up a mob that killed him. A mob who nailed him to the cross."

"They had a trial first." Grant liked his stories accurately told. "You remember about Pilate."

"They did have a trial but even after the disciples heard the sentence, they didn't quite believe that Jesus would be killed. He had talked so much of life. He had brought healing to so many. More than that, he was so very much alive himself. Probably he was one of the most 'alive' men who ever lived. Whenever he came among people they felt more alive themselves. They laid aside their sicknesses and worries. Jesus seemed to love all sorts of growing things and was always talking about them—trees and grain, birds and animals and certainly people. When he was sentenced to be nailed to a cross, the disciples couldn't take in the idea that he might soon be *dead*. And then that unbelievable day came so quickly when he was crucified and was indeed dead. His disciples were stunned, just as you and I would be if someone we loved were so tragically taken from us.

"For a while after that, the disciples couldn't do anything at all. They couldn't go back to their work. They couldn't talk about him, and they couldn't talk about anything else. There wasn't any point to anything. Jesus had furnished the ideas and the strength for all of them, and he was gone. They had had such a good time with him too, and now there wasn't anything to have a good time about. Still, all of his best friends kept getting together and talking.

"And then one day when they were together, one of them spoke up and said, 'We can't go on this way. He gave us work to do and we said we'd do it.'

"Another one said, 'People are still hungry and sick and unhappy. He'd be doing something about that.'

" 'But now he's gone,' said someone else. It seemed as if they couldn't get past that fact.

"Then the disciple who knew him best spoke up, 'If he were here, he'd say, "Don't be so cast down. God lives, doesn't he? The world is green and beautiful. The sun shines. Birds sing. If these things are true, it isn't fair to weep as if you'd come to the end of the world." I can almost hear him say such words.'

"Another disciple said, 'If he were here, he'd tell us to empty our pocketbooks onto the table, count out our money, and plan a trip for teaching.'

" 'By the way,' said a third disciple, 'where did I put that scroll of mine? The one I wrote his words on the day he talked to the crowd of five thousand people. I can't lose that.'

" 'He told me not to bother about writing down what he said,' someone else commented. 'He told me to remember as much as my heart could hold and that would be enough. And if he were here today, he'd say the same thing. Why, if he were standing there by that door— can't you see him?—he'd tell us that we didn't need any more of his words until we had used up the ones he had already given us. "Sufficient unto the day." Remember how he was always saying that?'

"The disciples chuckled out loud—the first time they'd laughed for days. 'You simply could not make him worry.

"Sufficient unto the day," he'd say, and then whittle away as if he didn't have a care.'

" 'I must say he did plenty of planning, though.' This remark from someone else. 'When he and I made that last trip across country, every time we sat down by the roadside to rest, he'd begin drawing a map in the dust with a stick and pointing out villages where he wanted to teach, and trying to decide which of us should go to which place.'

" 'And that's what he'd be doing this minute, if he were here.'

" 'If he were here, he'd make a plan. He'd send Andrew and Peter south again, probably, and James and John to the northwest.'

"Then I think John's face shone. 'I know exactly how he'd walk around this table giving one of us a set of directions, making a list of provisions for another, telling a third a new parable which any man would surely get the point of.'

" 'He'd stand right there and look at all of us and—'

"And then—or at least this is the way it seems to me—it seemed as if he *did* stand there. They remembered him so plainly. They heard his voice. They knew what he would say to them. They'd worked together so often before. Suddenly they knew they would always work together! You couldn't call a man like Jesus 'dead.' Not when his voice rang in your ears and his words rang in your heart. Not when you meant to spend all of your days to the end of them trying to make people understand what he meant by love for everyone. Probably he was the livest person in the room that minute."

Mother stopped abruptly. She brushed back her hair with her hand the way she always did when she was excited.

"That's it!" said Jim, standing right up at the table. "I see you do that—" he repeated her gesture—"I see you do that when you aren't here. When you go away I can't always remember what you look like if I just think, 'What does my mother look like?' But if I think of you in a special place saying some particular thing, then I can see you as plainly as if you were here. I can always remember the day you and I wired the back doorbell ourselves and you stood on a ladder brushing your hair out of your eyes just that same way."

"What *I* do when you go away—" Alberta spoke slowly—"is to go to sleep as if you had hold of my hand. If you're in the house, I can go to sleep by myself. But if you're gone, I can't bear to. I have to pretend you're in the room."

Grant picked up his fork and started on his cold potatoes. "What I do," he said, with his mouth too full, "is to try not to think of you at all. Because if I think of you, then I can't forget to bring in the wood for the fireplace and clean my fingernails, and things. But when you're gone I really remember you better than if you were here."

For Jim, the argument was not finished. "I guess you could say that Jesus in that way did rise from the dead."

"I'd say he never died," contributed Alberta cheerfully. "I'd say he just seemed dead for a while when his disciples were in the dumps."

"I'd say somebody ought to tell Grandmother the truth about it." This from Grant.

Mother hastened to protest. "But you can't say that any one person's ideas are more true than another's. This happens to be *my* idea. But it makes him more real to Grandmother to think about his rising from a tomb and being caught up into heaven. As indeed it must have done for the man who wrote the story which was finally put into the Bible."

"Probably it doesn't make a lot of difference," said Grant, "just so it works for you."

"Oh, no," cried Alberta in alarm. "I don't want to have the wrong idea about something and go on thinking it's the right idea. That's dreadful. Supposing I thought the world was flat."

"Try out your ideas. That's what Columbus did." Jim was triumphant. "Columbus thought the world was round, and he knew that if it was round then he could reach the east by sailing west. If he'd been wrong, he would have fallen off into space and then he'd know he had the wrong idea."

Grant protested. "That's a good way to try out ideas about sailing or ideas about keeping your airplane up in the air, but you can't try out an idea about will you live after you're dead. You can't come back and tell anyone else and no one can tell you. Now with some ideas, you just take 'em or leave 'em."

Alberta also protested. "Still I don't want the wrong idea. If it's true like Grandmother says, then I don't want to believe Mother's way. Mother's idea makes more sense to me, though, even if it isn't in a book."

Jim spoke slowly. "Well, there are some things you can't find an answer for in a book." He hesitated. "Although, of course, it's Grandmother's story that got written in about the best book there's supposed to be." Then he smiled. "Even if it's in a book, you've got to figure it out for yourself: was it that way or was someone trying to explain something which maybe he didn't completely understand himself?"

This conversation took place in an old white house on Eleventh Avenue in Ashland, Wisconsin. It was written down almost verbatim by the mother before the children's voices had died away for that night.

Another parent would have picked up Alberta's question, "Do you believe that Jesus rose from the dead?" in a different frame of mind and a different frame of reference. Even though she might believe that the physical body in a modern day is incapable of being brought back to life after it has died, still she would admit the miracle in the case of Jesus. Because the power of God is limitless and because Jesus partook of that power, it could have been possible—she would deduce—for his body to have been quickened into life again. With supernatural help he could roll away the stone from the tomb and walk abroad among his fellows, appearing and disappearing at will. This is part of the eternal mystery of God's having dwelt among men in the person of his Son. She might further declare, "I don't understand how there could be a resurrection, of course, but there are ten thousand things I don't understand. Every day, though, science is finding impossibilities to be possible. Perhaps some day we will understand even this greatest of all incredibilities. Actually I don't ask to understand. Who am I to read the mind of God? I accept the well-attested record: Jesus rose from the dead, disclosed himself to his disciples, and when he felt that they understood unforgetably that he was among them, then he ascended into heaven. I believe that his disciples could not so stanchly have affirmed seeing him if they had not actually seen him. Certainly they were not expecting to see him again, but there he was, among them. They were so sure that they had seen him that their contemporaries believed them. Since that day millions of men and women have believed, in faith, and I choose to take my place with the believing."

Still another parent, also believing that the disciples and many of those close to Jesus actually saw him among them after his death, would base the phenomenon upon a different concept of individuality. They would recall Paul's reference to the spiritual body, for instance, and point out that there have been many persons in all times and cultures who held that every physical body is interpenetrated by a body made of matter too high in vibration for ordinary sight to perceive under ordinary circumstances—an etheric body which is the real vehicle of the soul. It was this spiritual body, they would say, which was manifest to the disciples after Jesus' death. Having been dead for so short a time, Jesus could make use of some of the physical energy still clinging to the spiritual body, as it is said to do for a while, and could make himself plain to their sight. Then, when he was sure that they knew he still lived, he went on to another dimension of experience. "In my Father's house are many mansions" became a meaningful phrase for them after he had demonstrated the indestructibility of consciousness.

However parents may choose to interpret the life, death, resurrection, and message of Jesus, they have one inescapable fact with which to deal: those who wrote the record believed what they had heard and witnessed. His closest disciples believed it to be the heart of Jesus' teaching that God was a father wise and loving beyond human comprehension and always accessible, and that the Father expected his children to perfect their nature as his sons. They also believed that he exemplified in his own life the qualities he attributed to God. Those who knew him best believed that Jesus was the Messiah, the promised savior, the perfect son of man, peculiarly the son of God, and that he demonstrated everlasting life. As modern parents many may feel the necessity of arguing with the reported facts, but that the recorders believed their facts no one seems to doubt.

VI. What of Death?

I never spoke with God,
Nor visited in heaven;
Yet certain am I of the spot
As if a chart were given.

EMILY DICKINSON

"If a man die, shall he live again?"

Old as the race, the question rises freshly to the mind of each child. For him it is a new question and terrifically important. He is fortunate, probably, when it comes to him first as a speculative, impersonal question written across a far horizon. From the shelter of his family, it appears interesting but not threatening. The years will give him plenty of time, he feels, for weighing the answers. But some children run upon the question as upon the point of a sword. It is against such a possibility, before death stabs at personal security, that a parent can fortify his child by sharing something of his own feeling for the further outreaches of life.

The answer to the question, "If a man die, shall he live again?" has always been one of the concerns of religion. In rite and ceremony, primitive man made manifest whatever answer he had figured out. Civilized man does the same thing. And if he refuses to take part in rite and ceremony, his refusal is his answer also.

Although the Christian religion predicates a belief in life after death, there are few religious considerations on which there is less unanimity of opinion. Roman Catholicism teaches a fairly systematized theory of the reality of the soul; the importance of the individual's attitude at death; his forgiveness of his enemies and his acceptance of redemption; his dying in faith; his ensuing period of purgation and purification in purgatory; his subsequent descent into hell or ascent to heaven; teaches also the efficacy of the prayers of the living in behalf of the so-called dead. Protestantism teaches a variety of theories, ranging from the Roman to the strictly agnostic, i.e., the point of view that no one knows what happens after death, so let death be accepted as a physical fact.

The religious traditions of the East also offer their theories of death and immortality. By and large they come nearer to the Roman Catholic than to the general Protestant point of view, especially in acceptance of the genuine immortality of the soul, the importance of a good life to a happy ongoing, the aid which the living may give to the so-called dead.

Basic to any consistent theory of death and ongoing life is the question as to what is born when a new individual comes into this world. And the relatedness of the questions about the beginnings and endings of life seems more apparent, oddly, to children than to most ministers. But then in other ways children are often psychologically more mature than their dogma-ridden elders. Listen to the questions of a child of elementary school age when he is first probing considerations of death. Almost always he will ask in some form, "But what am I?" "Where did my soul come from in the first place?" "Where was it before I was born?" "Did I ever live on earth before?" "If my soul is eternal, like you say, what does it do without a body?"

No one can deal affirmatively with the general question of survival unless he has some clear idea of what, or who, comes into life, and some idea as to what constitutes human personality—the essential entity.

The biological answer we know, up to a point. We know something about the part played by the sperm and egg furnished by the parents, the number and the pattern of division of the chromosomes; we know a good deal about those infinitely tiny carriers of heredity called the genes; we know how an embryo develops, reaches readiness for birth, is born, and ensuingly grows to maturity. We also know that there is nothing permanent about the biological aspect of individuality; not merely in the sense that all life is impermanent and every individual must sometime die, but in the sense of constant change and replacement. Experts in food metabolism, utilizing radioactive particles and Geiger counters, have discovered the way in which food molecules enter a cell, replace some part of the cellular structure and leave again, replaced by other molecules, so that the entire body is in a constant state of dynamic change, and the molecular structure of the body is turned over at regular intervals.

The psychological answer as to what is born we also know up to a point. We know that mind and body appear to be a partnership (which we speak of as psychosomatic), the mind dependent upon the brain which acts as a clearing house for knowledge provided through the five senses. However, nowadays, many feel that there is carefully documented evidence to suggest that the mind may not be entirely dependent upon the brain. Scientists who have experimented with clairvoyance, clairaudience, precognition, psycokinesis and related factors feel that the mind at times acts independently of the five senses; that there appears to be an expanded consciousness which is not dependent upon the physical brain; indeed, that one function of the brain may be to strain out too much awareness of extra-sense phenomena and to restrict the mind's activities, for the most part, to sense data. In such a view the mind is primarily an attribute of the soul, or core-entity, which comes into the body at birth and is freed at death. Further, taking note of documentation on apparitions of the living and of the dead—manifestations of persons who are not in the geographical proximity of those who "see" them—they tend to conclude that the core-entity, the soul, has certain material properties of its own, probably being composed of very fine matter at a high rate of vibration which does not customarily register to the human eye. This finely constructed vehicle of the soul, some persons feel, is what St. Paul meant by the spiritual body. During life as we know it on earth, they hold, this spiritual body has close attachment to the physical body, although not always restricted to the physical body's spatial orientation, but at death it is entirely freed.

At some stage in a child's life, questions about the soul and ongoing life absorb his attention. And a parent has to answer in some fashion for the answers to such questions are the foundation upon which the superstructure of his life will be built.

Some parents answer, "These are questions to which we do not have certain answers. We cannot prove that the soul does not exist, but on the other hand there seems slender proof that it does. Psychologists have not shown that there is any important aspect of personality not accounted for by the mind dependent upon the brain which is its working organ. Hence there is nothing to live on after the body dies." Death, for parents of this persuasion, is a fact which cannot be evaded. The best they can do for their children is to temper the fact by the quality of their own acceptance.

"Will we ever see Mummy again?" begged little Marie, wiping her swollen eyes and clutching her father's hand.

"No, we won't see her again, Marie," her father answered through tight lips. "She is dead and she cannot come back."

"But can't we go where she is?"

"We don't know where she is, except that she is gone. Some day we will be gone, too."

"To some place we don't know about?" asked Marie hopefully.

"No, not gone to any other place. Just gone. When our bodies have finished their usefulness, they slowly turn into dust and are mixed with the earth. And that's the end, as far as we know." Her father felt that he should say something more and added, "Perhaps some of the dust which was once ourselves is used by the plants and trees which grow in the earth. I like to think so. Perhaps, as some scientists say, living matter is never completely lost. It just changes its form, the way hydrogen and oxygen may sometimes be water and sometimes steam and sometimes ice."

"But we won't see Mummy." The one stark fact obliterated all explanations for Marie. For her father, also, the fact blotted out every lesser matter. He had no words to ease the child's heart, but he held her closely.

Years later Marie remarks on that day: "My father gave me something then, when we clung to each other in our grief, that has comforted me more than any assurance of immortality. I think it was a kind of assurance of one human being's understanding of another, a thing so rare and wonderful that it makes all the rest of life worth living."

Edith Worley at fourteen seemed at once the most carefree and the most thoughtful youngster in her high school class. She was always aware of other people's needs, always—as her classmates said—"doing something for somebody." And yet she had plenty of time for her own

very active life. Her favorite pastime was riding a horse.
Almost every Saturday morning found her dashing cross-
country on Midnight, dark hair streaming in the wind. A
fence was nothing to Midnight, or to Edith. It anyone
remonstrated with her father over the girl's feats, he
would say, "Life is sweet. Sweet and hard. Edith's equal
to all of it. Let her ride."

Then one day when Midnight was trotting down a
peaceful lane, his foot slipped on a rock and for no
accountable reason he stumbled, reared back, and flung
Edith—expecting nothing and unprepared—upon a pile
of fence rails. Her back was broken.

For ten days in spite of the best care of a modern hospital staff she gasped for breath. Pain continually drove
her into unconsciousness from which she seemed to
emerge with increasing reluctance. One morning, at the
doctor's request, her father stood beside her bed and spoke
to her sternly. "Edith! Edith, you've got to hang on to
consciousness. Do you hear me? The doctors can't fight
for you unless you fight, too."

With an effort she looked up at him. "Will I ride
again, Father? Some day will I ride again?"

Her father did not hesitate. "No, Edith. As far as the
doctors can tell, you will never ride again."

"Will I walk?"

"No, you will not walk, either. Not unless a miracle
happens."

There was a faint smile on her face as she spoke. "We
don't believe in miracles, do we?"

"Not that kind." Then as she seemed slipping away
again, his voice became stern. "Edith, listen to me. You
have to take hold."

"Why? There's nothing to live for." Then she made
an effort to raise her head. "There's nothing to die for,

either, is there? We don't believe in life after death. I like living, you know."

Her father took the two limp hands firmly in his own. "Edith, listen to me. We have to live to the end of our strength—the strength of our bodies and the strength of our spirits. It's our compact with the people who come after us. There's no other way to pass on the courage that came to us from our forebears. Your great-great-grandmother was blind from her childhood but they say that a gayer, finer spirit never lived. You can't let her down. We Worleys stand up to life. Whatever comes after death—we let the future take care of that. We dare to let the future take care of itself because we live up to the present." He felt unhappily that his words sounded like quotations but he had to find some way to make the child understand. "Listen, Edith. I don't understand about dying and what comes after. But I've got a sure hunch that it matters a lot *how we live*."

Then Edith looked straight up at him, her young brown eyes searching the older eyes so like her own. "I understand you without any talk. It's all right. I'm living."

And Edith lived, long and merrily, as the neighbors for three counties around can testify. She never rode again. But one day there was a miracle of knife and bone and she did walk again. Walking, as she says, is a thrill her friends can never quite get the flavor of. The surgeon who performed the operation was astounded at its success. "I thought she'd walk, all right, but I never thought she'd stride!" Her stride is long and certain, free and firm. Like her life.

Some people, such as Edith and her father, find life condensed into an essence. For them, present responsibility has a quality which those who think in eons sometimes miss. Pleasure too—each day's joy—is tasted for its full flavor. This is what they have to pass on, and being individuals of integrity they do not try to pass on something else.

Perhaps the most defeating situation in which a parent finds himself is one in which he feels his own belief too stark for a child and tries therefore to affirm a conventional conviction about immortality which he does not hold. A mother, for instance, may comfort her young son in the loss of his father with words that attest eternal life, while she herself is mourning a husband irretrievably dead. Or a father may spin a tale of the heavenly happiness of the children's mother, while hopeless finality fills his own heart. In such cases the confused child, not able to bring awareness of the doubletalk to the surface, develops a double dread of death: he not only has panic over loss but also panic over the agonized reaction of the parent who is bereaved.

Some pragmatic parents, while not exactly believing in the survival of personality, operate on the theory that they have nothing to lose and perhaps something to gain in living, and answering, *as if* immortality were a fact.

It is more than two generations since Pete Peterson was ten years old and put his birthday pennies in the collection at Sunday school. Then he came home announcing, "I don't want immortal life."

"What do you mean, you don't want immortal life?" asked his Aunt Anna in astonishment.

"I mean that when I'm dead, I want to be dead. I want to live to be about as old as Grandpa Neilson and then when I die, I don't want to live forever."

His sister Hilda looked up with surprise. "Don't you want to remember things, or to think, or to know about your family, or *anything?*"

Pete shook his head. "When I'm dead, I don't care what

happens. They can chuck me to the wolves if they want to. Everybody can get drunk if they want to. Everybody can murder everybody if they want to. When I'm dead, I'm dead."

Then spoke Grandma Peterson. Her blue eyes snapped and she clicked off her words with precision made more emphatic by her Danish accent. "It's just for people like you that God Almighty gave us immortality! So that you *have* to care what happens after you're dead. You never saw a drunk man, Pete Peterson, but you know it's a dreadful thing and you're right. You never want to see one, not now nor after you're an immortal soul in glory. I don't hold traffic with the idea of leaning out of heaven to watch the wicked burn in hell, but I must say I'd do a lot of work in my day to keep from seeing the sons of men drunk after I've gone to my reward."

Pete Peterson is an old man himself now but he remembers his grandmother's words "as if they were yesterday." He says: "I never figured out to this day just what kind of immortality I believe in, but still I never got over the feeling Grandma Peterson put in me that if there might be the kind of immortality which allows for seeing how things are after death, then I want to be sure that the deeds of my living life won't rise up to wreck my immortal eyesight."

Sometimes parents find that children take their answers much more literally, or at least more wholeheartedly, than the parents take their own views, and that at a time when death puts the answer to the test, it may be the child who demonstrates the parents' conviction—or who turns a halfhearted opinion into a conviction.

Ronald and Rachel were twins, tall for twelve years, and as full of energy as an east wind. If they had not been quick at their lessons there would never have been any school work because neither of them had time to waste indoors. Then suddenly an epidemic of scarlet fever caught them both and the quarantine sign on the door spoke weeks of confinement.

They were very ill. Except in their concern for each other, they scarcely seemed aware of what went on. "How's Ronnie?" Rachel would ask the nurse or her mother. "Tell me about Rachel," Ronald would beg of them.

On the night when Ronald grew rapidly worse, Rachel seemed to sense the fact, although through her closed door she could not hear the coming of the doctors nor the summoning of her father. At midnight she spoke up firmly to the nurse keeping vigil beside her, "Please ask my mother to come here right away."

"She's busy," said the nurse. "Won't I do?"

"I know she's busy," said Rachel. "She's watching Ronnie die. Anyway, that's what you think she's doing. But she must come here now."

Her mother came. Rachel looked up at her anxious face. She spoke quickly because talking hurt her throat. "Listen, Mother, if Ronnie dies, do you believe that's the end of everything for him?"

"Of course not, darling," said her mother, leaning near and taking Rachel's hand in hers.

"We believe that Ronnie's soul goes out to some other place, but he's still Ronnie, isn't he? We believe that he keeps on growing, somehow. Maybe not the way we grow here on earth, but in some other way which God understands. We believe that, don't we?"

"Yes, we do," said her mother firmly.

"We believe that we'll go on living after we die, don't we? Somehow, some place, you'll be you and Father will be himself and Ronald will be Ronald. God has a plan and a place for all of us and it won't be any time at all until we're together again. That's what we think, don't we?"

"Yes, we do," said Mother again.

Rachel looked up into her mother's tired, drawn face and spoke sharply. "Then act like God was God and his plan was best. I bet it gives Ronnie fits to see all of you looking so worried. If I could go in there, I'd laugh at the idea that dying could make any difference between Ronnie and me. Ronnie'd laugh, too."

Whereupon Rachel turned over and went to sleep.

Her mother returned to Ronald's room. As she came in, everyone looked at her. Her face was serene. She spoke in a natural voice. "Constance," she said to one of the nurses, "I wonder if you'd scurry up some sandwiches and coffee."

"My dear," said Father in bewilderment, "this is no time—"

"Yes, it is," said Mother quietly. "We haven't eaten all day and that's not right. We need our strength." She stood at the foot of the bed looking down at the boy.

Ronald opened his eyes and smiled faintly. "I feel better now. I'm not so smothered now." He drew a deep breath and fell into a natural sleep.

Afterwards one doctor said, "I didn't think he could possibly open that throat to speak again."

The other doctor said, "It doesn't make sense, with that racing heart."

Mother said—with what seemed to the doctors considerable irrelevance—"Bless her heart, she *believes* her beliefs."

Still later, in their own room, Father said, "How is Rachel? What did she want with you?"

"She's asleep," said Mother, beginning to brush her hair.

"She just wanted to tell me that immortality isn't merely a doctrine. She said it was a fact to act upon. She said that if we believed the soul was immortal and had ages ahead for its perfecting, why then it was selfish to grieve when it merely passed from one state to another. She said there was something grand and triumphant about some of the family's going ahead and others of us coming on. She said it made us think in longer terms than our little lifetimes and that we gathered a kind of cosmic courage into ourselves when we made room for the death which is only transition. She said it must be terribly hard for God when faith gives way to apprehension, and that a Christian ought to act like a Christian because it wasn't as if no one had gone before to show us the way."

Father interrupted. "It doesn't sound like Rachel to say all that."

"She used other words. But that was her idea: immortality is a fact to act on."

Some parents feel they have a much stronger word to say about ongoing life in the light of the findings of extra-sensory perception. They point to carefully recorded instances of apparitions, both of the living and of the dead, as tentative proof of the viability of the etheric or spiritual body, the vehicle of the soul; to the ability of the mind, apparent in much experimentation and in many spontaneous instances, to "see" clairvoyantly and to "hear" clairaudiently, even to foretell, as evidence of the mind's independence of the five senses and perhaps of the physical body. With experimentation in the whole psychic field growing both more widespread and more careful, they feel the accumulation of evidence should be made available to young people interested in investigating the question of immortality.

" 'If a man die, shall he live again?' "

"My child, it seems to me—this way—but others feel—"

Immortality, in the mind of small children, is not concerned with human beings alone. There is the important question of their pets. What of the dog poisoned through someone's carelessness? The kitten who wanders away and never comes back? The canary, the pony, the rabbit?

Edwin and his spaniel Bridget were born on the same day and so, as Edwin would gravely explain, "it's different than with most boys and dogs." For more than five years they had been inseparable companions indoors and out.

One weekend Mother and Father both went away on a trip and Great-aunt Hester came to look after Edwin and Bridget. Aunt Hester did not know a great deal about small boys but anything she lacked in imagination she made up in good will and meticulous care. Edwin had never been so promptly dressed and fed and read to. Bridget, too, had exactly the right food at exactly the hour mother had marked on her schedule. Aunt Hester remembered everything except Bridget's fondness for open gates and the fact that even a shut gate did not keep her in unless the latch were tightly snapped. So on Saturday afternoon Bridget got out into the alley. A coal truck . . . the driver did not see Bridget . . . and the next thing Aunt Hester knew she was standing in the back yard looking into the contorted face of a small boy who, in turn, looked down incredulously at his dead dog.

After the first dreadful hour when the veterinary had taken Bridget away and Aunt Hester had telephoned the news to Father, the questions began. "Where did Bridget's soul go, Auntie? Has she gone to heaven?"

"My goodness, no child. Dogs don't go to heaven."

"Where do they go, then? Auntie! You don't mean

that Bridget's dead forever? You don't mean we'll never
see her again?"

"There, there, child. Your daddy will get you another
dog."

Small comfort to a boy of five. Another dog? As well
another world entirely. "I don't want another dog.
Bridget was my dog. Where is she now?"

"She's dead, darling. There, there. Dogs have to die."

"So do people die but then they go to heaven. Why
isn't Bridget in heaven?"

"The Bible doesn't say anything about animals in
heaven. There wouldn't be room in heaven for all the
animals. You can see that."

Edwin stood squarely before his aunt, feet spread apart,
hands behind him, a look of stubborn bewilderment on his
face. "Then I'm not going, either."

"Edwin! When you get there, everything will be so
nice that you won't mind about not having Bridget."

"I'll always mind about not having Bridget." His chin
quivered again. "And if God hasn't got room for dogs,
I'll be bad all my life so he won't let me in."

"You mustn't say things like that." She tried to draw
Edwin into her lap. "There's a difference between
humans and dogs."

Edwin maintained his stance. "I know there's a difference. Dogs have four legs and people have two legs. People sleep in beds and dogs sleep in baskets. But dogs can
play and have fun, can't they? Dogs can love you and
stick by you. Why Bridget—" He stopped. There wasn't
any use.

It was nearly midnight when Father drove in. Edwin,
sleeping fitfully, heard the car on the driveway. He
might have known his father would come back. He

scrambled out of bed and by that time his father was coming through the bedroom door followed by Aunt Hester. Edwin jumped into his father's arms and neither of them said anything. They just hugged each other. Finally Edwin slid down from his father's arms. "It's tough, isn't it?" he said. "It's tough that nobody could bark when you drove in."

"You bet it's tough, son."

"Father, she didn't go to heaven." Edwin reached desperately for his father's hand when he heard himself saying the words. "She's dead but God didn't want her."

"Who says she didn't go to heaven?" asked father sternly.

"Auntie says that heaven is no place for animals. It doesn't say a thing about them in the Bible."

"Oh, that—" Father dismissed the matter with a gesture. "It doesn't have to say anything about them in the Bible because it says that God is our Father and we expect a father to look after his children's dogs and other pets."

"Edwin!" Aunt Hester was speaking to the senior Edwin now and her tone was severe. "You're talking about Holy Writ."

"Nonsense," said Father, patting Aunt Hester's shoulder. "You'd look after a puppy in need any time one came your way, my dear. I'm just allowing God to be as friendly as we humans are."

Then Father turned to Edwin, speaking seriously. "I don't understand a lot about heaven, son, except that I believe that whatever happens after we're dead is all right. Do you know what I mean? It may be all different from anything we know now. But whatever it is, God will do the right thing by all of us. Men, women, boys, girls, babies, dogs—everybody. After all, if God is love, we don't have to be anxious about his taking care of us. That's the way I see it."

"Oh." Edwin looked at his father's face intently. Evidently he was satisfied with what he saw there for he climbed into his bed again.

His father tucked the covers under his chin. "Tomorrow we'll talk about it some more. We're sure going to miss little Bridget, but wherever she is, it's okay with her."

"Okay," said Edwin, drawing a long breath which was both a spent sob and a yawn. He could go to sleep now, really to sleep, and figure out the rest in the morning. Tomorrow he'd miss Bridget just as much, but he could stand missing her if everything was okay with Bridget.

It would seem unnecessary that so many children must wait until calamity forces their parents to some sort of declaration on a philosophy of life after death. After all, the fact is always at hand and it might as well be accepted with serenity and dignity and common sense as left to an emotional crisis. Not so many years ago, a great many people refused to speak of life insurance in tones above a whisper. Husbands, in broaching the subject to their wives, were met with a frantic, "Don't talk about it, darling. I can't even bear to think of such a thing." Pedagogical salesmanship has helped to recondition thousands into a more sensible attitude. A little more pedagogy is in order on the whole subject of helping children to meet the fact of death. Certainly those who believe that death is only an incident in the long life of the soul should be able to speak not only triumphantly but, in a sense, casually. And those who hold that death is life's supreme adventure can share their courage and curiosity in conversations by the way. Fear of death probably saps more of the world's creative energy than any other fear, and those who have achieved a philosophy which dissipates that fear have something important to share with their fellows.

Children like to speculate. The future looms so large before them, the years from eight to eighty stretch so endlessly into the future, that they feel a genuine impersonality in their speculations. Many a parent has been momentarily startled to hear his small son's cheerful question, "Now when you die, Daddy, what kind of a funeral do you think you'll have?" Or his daughter's hopeful demand, "After you're dead, can this picture be mine to keep?" Such offhand questions are a ready-made lead into common-sense family discussion of the practical considerations involved in funerals, in burial, in customs of mourning, as well as in the immortality of the soul.

The parent who can "condition" his child so that death appears at least as a door ajar through which honest questions dare peer into the future has probably rendered his child a larger service than the parent who writes any kind of final answer to placard upon a door tightly closed.

VII. What of Prayer?

He led them then into another room, where was a hen and chickens, and bid them observe a while. So one of the chickens went to the trough to drink, and every time she drank she lifted up her head and her eyes towards heaven. "See," said he, "what this little chick doth, and learn of her to acknowledge whence your mercies come, by receiving them with looking up."

JOHN BUNYAN (*Pilgrim's Progress*)

There are two sorts of homes in which children are not likely to ask questions about prayer: homes in which prayer is a patent absurdity, and homes in which prayer is taken for granted. But a great many children grow up in homes which fall some place between these two categories, and these children are likely at some time to ask a good many questions about prayer.

Their questioning may come suddenly when some untoward incident makes them suddenly aware of their own prayers.

"But I prayed, mother. I prayed every day, a lot of times every day." Barry's voice betrayed incredulous disappointment. This was his birthday, his seventh birthday, the day to which he had looked forward so eagerly and from which he had expected so much. In spite of planning to be up with the sun, he had overslept and had almost been late for breakfast. When he bounded into the sunny dining room, there by his place at the table were packages of all sizes and shapes. True to the family tradition, he opened only the smallest one before he ate. It was a key ring just like Father's. He smiled triumphantly. Of course, a key ring. He would have to have keys because the Thing he was waiting for—the biggest present of his life so far— would need to be chained to the fence and locked just like a bicycle when he went to play with Jack or Raymond. He laughed aloud. His mother laughed and his father laughed. Millie, the cook, stuck her head in the doorway; laughed, too, long and heartily. No doubt Millie was in on the secret. He hoped she hadn't seen the Thing because he wanted to watch her tongue pop out like her eyes when she realized what she was looking at. Thinking about Millie's surprise made it hard to listen to what his father was saying, although everyone was being ever so jolly.

"I'm glad you're here," Barry said to his father, beamingly. He wanted everyone to share the big moment. "I'm glad no one got sick in the night and called you out." Ordinarily it would be his mother who was more thrilled than anyone over a big surprise, but this was something different. No doubt his father would even want to run the Thing. Well, he could. It was plenty big if his father didn't mind being squeezed up a bit.

After breakfast, Barry unwrapped the other presents. It was great of Uncle Tom to send him the little kodak. Ordinarily a kodak would have occupied him for a long time. It was great of his father and mother to get him such a swell set of tools, but he wished they hadn't. Vaguely he felt that they really couldn't afford the Thing and then all these tools besides. Anyway he wouldn't have much time for tools now. He hoped his father wouldn't mind carpentering alone in the hobby hour which they tried to spend together just after dinner.

Pretty soon everything was unwrapped and Barry had said all the "thank you's," folded all the papers, and stood tremblingly beside the door which led into the garden.

"My stars, I never saw you so excited, Barry," said his mother, patting the dark head.

"It's something to be seven years old, eh, son?" said Father, starting for the living room.

"I'm ready now," said Barry. The moment had come and there was no use waiting longer. In fact he couldn't wait longer. "I'm ready now."

"Ready for what?" asked Mother, mystified by his great eagerness.

"You know for what!" laughed Barry. "Let's go together."

After that, Barry didn't know what was said. It seemed as if he had stood in the doorway for long dizzy hours trying to understand their words but never really believing them at all. At first it was a joke they were making . . . the joke was too long . . . then it wasn't a joke at all . . . they were surprised he had ever expected the Thing . . . it hadn't even seriously entered their minds. A toy automobile the size of the one at the Fair, with an engine and all those gadgets—why, the Thing cost hundreds of dollars.

"Hundreds of dollars?" cried Barry. "But hundreds of dollars are nothing to God."

He had *prayed* for that automobile. He had prayed believingly. Not a shadow of doubt had crossed his mind. He had been good for weeks, even in little things his mother would never know the difference about, such as brushing his teeth after breakfast. He had been good and he had prayed. And God — what had God done? He had paid exactly no attention at all. What kind of God is that who doesn't answer the prayers of the good and believing?

This proved to be one morning when Father's patients waited in the office and Mother's painting waited in the studio, and Millie had the same answer for all telephone calls: "If you will call again at noon, please." Father and Mother knew a major crisis when they met it. Afterwards they said to each other, "If we had only known he was praying and expecting." But Barry had felt that the proof of his faith was not to mention the automobile in the prayers he said aloud. And now he was through with praying. Through with God, too, for God the Almighty who could do anything he wanted — make a world and raise the dead — God hadn't even bothered to listen about the little car.

"Barry, I have a question to ask you," said Father after they had gone into the living room and were sitting before the fire which Mother had lighted on the hearth. Barry, hunched on a footstool, waited. "If you were sick in bed with a bad case of measles and asked me for a piece of mince pie and I wouldn't give it to you, would you think I was just being mean?"

"Nope," said Barry, shaking his head. That was a silly question. "No, I wouldn't," he repeated.

"You would believe that I knew more about the measles and pie and small boys than you did, wouldn't you?"

"I'd know you didn't want to make me sicker. But I'm not sick and an automobile isn't like pie. An automobile would only make me happy and not hurt anyone."

"Then let's put it this way," said his father gently. "You don't know what's good for you. Not completely. I don't always know what's good for me. We just aren't wise enough. But even if what we asked for might not do us harm, there's still the possibility that we might be asking more than our share. We can't even guess all the considerations God has to take into account when he considers the desires of our hearts. Isn't that true?"

Barry nodded. What his father said was plain enough.

"Now take your automobile. You prayed for it, but you didn't expect God to drop an automobile from the clouds. He works pretty much through natural laws and situations. If you were to get that automobile, I'm the one who would have to pay for it. That particular car cost close to a thousand dollars if it costs a cent. It was a show car and a marvel of mechanics. I don't have a thousand dollars to spend. In order to buy that car I'd have to borrow money on my insurance, which would be a foolish thing to do, or we'd have to cancel our order for coal and live in a cold house all winter, and not buy any winter clothes. We couldn't even buy gas for the car we now have and I'd lose a great deal of time trying to reach my patients by streetcar. God knows all these things. When you ask for a car, he has to consider everybody who would be concerned with getting the car."

Barry stuck to the point about the money. "Supposing Mother got sick," he said. "Supposing she had to be sent on a trip like Mrs. Perkins. You'd find the money fast enough. You'd ask God to help you find the money. We all would."

"You bet I'd ask him," Father admitted. "I'd expect him to send me patients who could pay me so that I'd get the money. I'd expect him to give me better ideas than I'd ever had before so that I would be worth more money. But that's different, Barry. When it comes to your mother's health, we wouldn't care what we had to do without. But to do without food or clothes to buy put his feeling into words — ready for whatever came next.

Sometimes a child's having his prayers answered exactly as he wants them answered is an even more difficult experience to explain.

Kim was six the Christmas he got a wonderful sled, a sled which all but made up for his Mother's spending the holiday in a hospital with his new baby brother. However, that Christmas was not a white one and the sled had nothing to slide on. Christmas night Grandfather put Kim to bed. Just as Kim knelt down he asked, "Would it be all right to pray for snow?"

Grandfather thought it over, and the answer he gave made room for God's knowledge as to whether more or less snow were currently needed on the land, whether some people's need of snow were greater than others' need for dry open roads. It was all right, he thought, to ask God to send snow if it seemed best for the most people, if Kim could pray "Thy will be done."

So Kim thought over what Grandfather had said. Then he remarked judiciously, "I have been quite good and I think God would like to do it for me if he could." So he prayed; he really prayed with rousements for heavy snow, sufficient for the best of sledding. And in the night the snow came, blankets of it, one of the heaviest snows in years. Kim's delight in his sled was only exceeded by his approval of God.

That night he knelt again to say his prayer, his grandfather again standing by. ". . . . and give my baby brother a lot of muscle. . ." Kim went on. Then he raised his head. "Anything you'd like, Grandfather?"

Now that Grandfather had some real discussion on his hands to dissipate the private wire theory. It is easy for a child who finds his requests answered to conclude that make mistakes, but most of the time we think he acts wisely, don't we?"

"Yes, we do," said Barry.

"It seems to me we trust God's love and wisdom in much the same way. Sometimes I don't understand his action but I've learned confidence in him."

His mother spoke as if she had really tried things out with God.

His father said, "Either we have to believe that he cares for each one of us and will do that thing that is best for us and withhold the things which are not best for us, or we must believe that we simply do not matter in the eyes of God."

"Maybe we don't," said Barry.

"My own experience indicates that we do," said Father. "I think that the Maker of the universe is very much concerned with man. He has a plan for his children. If he forced us into that plan, then we wouldn't be the sons of God. We'd be merely puppets. No doubt his plan is all about us, plain enough. But we have to find it by using our own minds and hearts. We'll make ten thousand mistakes, just as men have made in the past, but we hope we are working a bit nearer to the plan with each generation."

Barry looked at his father wonderingly. "Do you believe God has a plan for me?"

"Yes, I do, son. I believe that if you listen closely enough and don't hurry or insist on the plan's being carried out your way, then the plan will come plain to you. Now take the way I stumbled into medicine. It might have looked as if I found my profession by accident, but I don't believe there was any accident about it. I believe I was led to it at the right time. Somehow when I was growing up it never occurred to me to be a doctor. During high school I concluded I'd go into the hardware business with my dad but I never was much elated over the idea. When I was a freshman I thought I'd be a lawyer. One summer I tried playground work in a settlement house. By the time I was a junior, I'd tried a lot of things. They all seemed okay but none of them interested me much. It began to worry me not to know what my profession was going to be. When I worried, I lost my appetite and got thin. Finally I was in such a miserable state that I went to a doctor. Old Dr. Hewitt. I went to him because my father always thought a lot of him. After he had reassured me about my health, he talked to me. He took me over to the hospital and showed me around. By the end of that afternoon I was a full-fledged doctor — all except going to medical school and interning and a few such little things. My mind was made up. Doctoring was *my* job. Simple as that."

Mother had a question. "Hadn't you ever prayed to be shown your job?"

"Sure, I had," Dad told her. "At first I prayed regularly in words, in special words I'd made into a special prayer. Then I quit using words and just kept on longing."

" 'Prayer is the soul's sincere desire, uttered or unexpressed.' " Barry knew that his mother was quoting. "Probably God isn't so very dependent upon our words. I suspect our words are more useful to us than to him because when we put our ideas into words we think them more clearly, and the clearer our ideas get, the easier it is for us to understand God's answer."

His father turned back to Barry, speaking gravely. "There isn't a lot one person can say to another when it comes to this business of prayer. But it seems to me that you hardly want to discard it until you've given it a little

more trial. It takes some time to learn to want wisely.
I'd experiment a little more if I were you."

Barry had been thinking his own thoughts while he listened to his parents. "It's okay about the automobile," he
said. "Prob'ly Jack and Raymond would feel kind of left
out if they didn't have automobiles, too. Prob'ly we'll go
racing our wagons some more. It's okay." Thus prag-
matically Barry disposed of the matter and reached for
his new kodak.

Had the whole discussion been over his head? Not at
all. Most of the ideas he understood, but more important,
he understood that his parents believed in the love and
wisdom of God. He understood, too, that his parents
thought it was important to know about God, to trust
him, to find his will. But above all else, Barry had the
feeling that God had never let his parents down and that
they expected to go right on keeping as near to God as
they could. They must have thought it was quite important for him to understand how they felt or his father would never have put off going to the office.

Barry wound the film into his new kodak, exactly the
way he had seen Jack wind his. It really was all right
about the automobile. It really was all right about God.
He would keep on praying; he hoped God did have a plan
for him. He hoped he'd find it. He hoped his father and
mother would live until he himself was an old, old man,
and that Millie would always be their cook. Having thus
taken care of eventualities, he went out to play like the
normal growing child he was. Years later he knew this
had been a big day in his life, although he never remembered what his parents had said. It was the day which
might have left him feeling cheated by life, defiant against
his disappointment, finished with prayer and skeptical
about the future. Instead, it left him — although he never

a toy might risk our health. There's a good deal of responsibility in handling money, you know. We aren't free to take money from a necessary thing just for our own pleasure."

"I know that," said Barry. "I wouldn't expect God to take the money that some sick person ought to use to go to the hospital. But some kids get those cars. Why couldn't I be one of them?"

"I don't know, Barry. No one knows the answer for sure, but there are a lot of possible reasons. For instance, it's a lot easier to ride around in a little car, especially such a honey of a car, than to take your tools and go make a box for a wagon and learn how to put on the wheels by yourself. And yet in the end you might be much happier to know how to use the tools. There may be a time coming in your life when you will need to know how to use tools. Or there may be some other reason why the car is not a good thing for you. Perhaps if you had the car, you couldn't put your mind on your school work which you really need to do after all you missed last spring. There are a great many possible reasons why it may not have been best for you to have that car. We don't know the reasons but since God didn't send the car, I believe the reasons are good ones which he knew about and considered."

Now Mother spoke for the first time. "Barry, you never doubt your father's love for you, do you? Even when he cannot stay home to play with you, even when he punishes you, you never doubt he loves you, I know."

"I know he loves me," said Barry.

"Most of the time, you trust his wisdom, too, don't you?" Mother seemed to be caring a lot for what she was saying. "He's only human, we know, and he can he is favored of God; that there must be something specially acceptable about his conduct to receive such obvious divine blessing. He has come upon a half-truth, i.e., that right relationship with God does indeed incline one's affairs to move smoothly, because in being 'right' with God one tends also to be in right relationship with his fellows. But it is treacherously easy for the child to settle for a small transformation in his circumstance rather than pushing on to a large transformation in himself. Some parents are acutely aware of this danger of successful petition.

Other parents overlook the word of caution because they themselves may be arrested at the favorite-son stage of spiritual development. For example, a father may discover that in the practice of prayer he releases untapped sources of power, of energy, of assurance, of mental alertness, of inner peace. He feels that he is in right relationship to the Source of the abundant life, and as a consequence of his constant renewal, he is able to manage his affairs more successfully. His circumstances greatly improve. His conclusion may then be that God has singled him out as a demonstration of the reward due to the righteous; that all he may thereafter undertake will be blessed. Hence he may level off at a relatively low spiritual plane, content to accept improvement in circumstances as the aim of prayer. Actually outward prosperity may indicate a mistaking of by-product for end, a lack of sensitivity to to the needs of others, an addiction to using God's power for one's own purposes rather than for transforming character into the likeness of God. It is a delicate matter, for parent or child, constantly to be checking performance, including circumstance and situation, against the nature of God as best a human being can sense his nature to be. It means constant appraisal of one's sensitivity as God's

instrument in meeting the needs of others, constant checking of one's own spiritual growth — and all this without
becoming centered on one's self. A parent can pass on
only as much as he knows of this ever-demanding process.

Children who become interested in prayer, sooner or
later become curious about the psychological processes
at work. Adolescents especially press for its justification
in modern terms. "What really happens when I pray? I
don't want to spend my time on something that isn't
reasonable. Even if I grant that some people get answers
to prayer, where do these answers really come from?
And how do they come about?"

To such questions it is not enough to say, "There are
states of consciousness in which man's experience outruns
his explanations," even though this is an obvious fact.
These children need a tentative explanation, a basis for
their experimentation, for they are likely to become the
ravelers of the world's mysteries. Some among them may
be the men and women who will wrest further secrets
from interstellar space, from the heart of the atom, from
the living chemistry of the blood, from the frontiers of
psychology. Almost every parent has a point of view
about prayer, although he may never have put it into
words until pressed by a young inquirer.

Mary stopped suddenly in the midst of a Chopin prelude
which she had been playing with apparent absorption. She
often played for a half-hour before dinner while her father sat in his favorite chair with the newspaper still un-
folded on his knee, just listening.

"Father, it's a funny thing about Mr. Ryerson." She
spoke quickly as if releasing thoughts long bottled up in
her mind. "I've thought about it before but I never knew
how odd it was until today."

"I don't know anything so funny about Mr. Ryerson,"

said her father with a smile which seemed as much for Mr.
Ryerson as for Mary. "I've always thought he was a pretty grand old man. Prince of the city fathers."

"Yes, I know he's grand. They said out at the Home
today that he has placed over twenty thousand children
in the Home and that he's never let one leave without a
real home or a job."

"I guess that's true all right."

"This afternoon he talked to all the high school seniors
who go out there to help with the recreation and story
hours. He said that for thirty years the Home had been
run on prayer. Then we got to talking about prayer and
John Addams came right out and said that he had heard
that Mr. Ryerson didn't even believe in God. And Mr.
Ryerson said he didn't believe in the kind of God most
people believed in, but that he believed in prayer. He
believed that when we pray in need, we do honestly
receive answers but that our prayers are heard by human
ears and our answers are delivered by human hands and
feet. Does that make sense to you?"

"It makes quite a bit of sense to me," said her father
slowly. "I know Mr. Ryerson never thinks of starting or
closing the day without a whole hour of silence. I've
known him when he was faced with tremendous problems, when a mortgage was about to be foreclosed on his
big farm back of the Home and his creditors literally
waited at the door; when the scarlet fever epidemic
swooped down on the place; when the near-by public
school was about to refuse to take his orphans without
tuition because so many of them came from out of the
state. But I've never known him to miss that hour of
silence no matter who was waiting to talk about what.
I've asked him about it once or twice." Father stopped
short.

Mary left the piano and came over to sit near him. "Go on."

"I'm not so good at explanations as he is. But the gist of what he says is that when he is completely quiet in body and mind, then the noise and petty problems of the day recede before the stillness of his deep desire, and help rises up from the recesses of his mind, probably from his memory."

"What on earth do you mean — help from his memory?"

"He means that during his life he has had many fine experiences with friends, with books, with people he may never have met personally but has heard about and admired. All of us have countless friends of this sort, in real life and in books, who have been our living companions and have stirred our imaginations. All these companions together have a rather tremendous amount of wisdom. We may have forgotten them, but deep in our minds they have made their imprint nevertheless. Now Mr. Ryerson says that when he sits in silence and spreads out his problems before all these wise and capable and generous people he has known, he feels just as if he were looking into the faces of a mighty audience before whom he wanted to lay a problem which they could decide and act upon. In an audience one doesn't see individual faces but the audience has personality none the less. It responds. And just as a reaction comes back from an audience so that a speaker is inspired to say things he never thought of before, and to use words he didn't realize were in his vocabulary, and to feel power surging in him which ordinarily he just does not have — so in confronting these unseen friends, he also has the sense of dealing with a great reservoir of wisdom and common sense and power. He begins to get ideas. His mood begins to change.

Anxiety gives way to peace, doubt to security, fear to confidence. He is more than his ordinary self."

"Maybe it's a kind of self-hypnosis."

"What if it is? It works. He goes into the silence asking for help, and he comes out having received the help. His perspective has widened and his mind has become more inventive. Sometimes he sees the next step clearly. Sometimes he doesn't see the next step at once but he has insight into what really caused his difficulty and then he knows that a solution is going to be possible.

"Well, for goodness' sake, Father, if that is as good psychology as it sounds, you'd think hundreds of people would try it because Mr. Ryerson just about does perform miracles."

"Hundreds of people don't try it because it takes tremendous self-control to spend two hours out of every day in honest-to-goodness meditation. Most of us couldn't even bear two hours of complete silence without trying to think. And you must remember that he doesn't do this meditating only when he is stuck with a big problem. He does it every day. Usually at least one of the hours is in his room, but he often walks through his wood-track or down the riverbank. All his boys and girls and his friends know about his need for silence and if he meets one of them and raises his hand in quiet salute, they pass on without speaking."

"I should think a person would feel silly just to sit down in a chair and start to meditate."

Her father smiles. "Not silly so much as empty. A lot of us haven't cultivated very wise and resourceful friends, either in real life or in books. We don't have a lot to turn to or to meditate about."

Mary sat silent a minute or two and then said, "I don't think I'd know how to meditate. And do you mean that

Mr. Ryerson could get answers to all his problems if he just meditated and never mentioned them out loud to anyone?"

"I doubt it. And I don't think he'd claim to. Probably he would get more answers than most of us because he has this superb discipline of mind. But he lets people know his problems, too. He asks for money and he asks for help. He goes after what he has to have."

"*That* kind of prayer is heard by human ears and answered by human hands and feet and tongue, I'll admit myself."

"Asking other people directly is probably part of the praying process. I used to be amused by the stories of the great old man of Bristol who ran his scores of orphanages 'by direct reliance upon prayer.' He said that he had no other means of support for his vast number of dependents. He made many a speech and wrote many a letter about his direct and single-minded reliance upon prayer. But he never seemed to realize that every time he spoke he was letting people know about the need of those children and the fact that he had no regular support for them. In a sympathetic world, such faith does not go unrewarded. Of course he found checks in his mail, wagonloads of food at his door, orders for clothing to his credit just when his resources were exhausted."

"However you explain it, his prayers were answered, too, though."

Again her father smiled. "Surely they were. Some will say that God, anticipating his need, planted the answer in human hearts so that it arrived right on time. Mr. Ryerson would say that people were told of a genuine need and they responded. And in both cases, it isn't beside the point that a man's consecrated, unpretentious life had something to do with the answers to his prayers."

"Mr. Ryerson's idea seems more reasonable to me, but harder."

"Why harder?" Her father looked quizzically at Mary.

"Why, if you have the old-time idea of God who is omnipotent and mighty and all that, you don't have to spend so much time reading great books and getting wise friends. You can just leave the ideas and the answers to God. He can look after people himself."

"I'm afraid you're mistaken, Mary. As far as I know all great men of prayer have also been men of disciplined lives. They seem to work unremittingly to find what they feel to be God's will and then to carry it out. Remember St. Francis and the Little Brothers and the way they served the entire countryside — lepers, rich men, peasants, scholars, birds, donkeys, the greatest and the humblest, anyone in need. The hours they spent on their knees were matched by hours of firsthand service. I must admit that it seems to be the case with all who have been great in prayer, however they explain their prayers."

Mary thought over what her father had said, got up from her chair, smiled at her father and commented in her practical fashion, "I guess if there is a God — I mean the kind of God most people have in mind when they say 'God' — why, he won't mind our trying to figure things out and explain them. And explain him too, if we can."

"I don't think he would mind. After all, we are said to be made in his image."

The dinner bell rang and the conversation changed to other matters. Nor has it been resumed in the months which have followed. But Mary's father has noticed that ever since that conversation her alarm has been ringing a quarter of an hour earlier than was formerly its custom. Perhaps Mary is experimenting on her own theory of prayer but whether it is Mr. Ryerson's theory or some other, her father doesn't know. He does not intend to ask. In her own time Mary will probably make her own comments on her own conclusions.

Another kind of parent, personally unconcerned with whatever psychological processes may be at work in prayer, might say flatly, "I don't think we are supposed to understand the process at work in prayer. It's enough to know that things are changed by prayer. Thousands in every generation have found this true: God answers. So accept the fact in faith. We have to accept many experiences on faith."

But a parent interested in observing what appears to be a process at work, at least in the case of intercessory prayer, may offer a third response. "It looks as if the mind of the one praying reached the mind of the one prayed for."

"Do you mean mental telepathy?" the young inquirer may ask.

"Something on that order. Let's say you are in trouble and I decide to pray for you. I focus my thought upon you and ask God to give you aid. Your mind picks up my strong intent and realizes the genuineness of my purpose. Your mind also takes it in that I believe there are tremendous resources available to you. And so your mind takes a fresh hold on these resources, whether of bodily health, mental peace, improvement in circumstances, or whatever it may be."

"Then prayer *is* a kind of thought exchange," the young inquirer insists.

"That and more. Let's take another example. A friend of mine has a son named Alan who is about to marry a girl who seems very much the wrong choice. I know my friend prays for his son. He probably says something like ... 'O God, give Alan wisdom. Let him realize how much this girl has to develop before their marriage could endure. Help him to face his future. May thy will be made perfect in his life.' Now I think the boy hears that prayer, especially if the father prays while the boy is asleep. On waking the boy brings to consciousness the thought, 'Maybe we should wait a while.' Or perhaps he thinks, 'It's true she has a long way to go, and so have I. If we face our shortcomings, maybe we can help each other.' Either way, he is in a new frame of mind and sees the situation differently from the way it appeared to him before the prayer was raised in his behalf. He 'got' his father's thought, as we say, but his father's prayer was something more than thought control. When his father addressed the source of all wisdom and love, he brought into play a quality of consciousness larger, wiser, more compassionate than his own. This greater consciousness, the supreme wisdom, is here in the universe, available. You could almost say that one person tunes in on it in behalf of another. And surely prayer is not less holy because it operates on laws which may some day be entirely understood by the mind of man."

The young inquirer may press further. "But do you think that most of us pray for the will of God to be done, no matter what the consequence to us or to the person we care about? Don't we usually pray for what looks best to us?"

"Of course we do, but to the degree that we want our own way, our prayer falls short of full efficacy. We're likely to pray, 'God, keep Johnny from buying a car, even if he has earned the money himself; he's too young for a rattletrap,' rather than, 'Make it plain to me if Johnny should have a car, and plain to him if he shouldn't.' We pray, 'Make Mary get in on time tonight. That's a fast crowd, God...' and we're likely to add to ourselves, 'and besides, it isn't fair to keep me awake worrying.' A truer prayer might be, 'Dear God, forgive my poor parenthood and lead Mary in your way.' We pray, 'Let Matilda pass her examination,' rather than, 'If Matilda needs to learn a lesson here, give us both strength to accept what we need, Father. Send what is best.' The difference is vast between wish-thinking in the terms of prayer and actually offering a situation, or a beloved person, to the care and wisdom of God, pledging ourselves to further his will as it is made plain."

This matter of the will of God gives some children much concern. A modern child is not conditioned to accept unquestioningly the will of his human parents, and no more does he bow to the idea of God's will without questioning God's character, his power, and his way of bringing his will to pass. "If God is good, how can he let so many poor people go hungry?" "If God loves us, like you say, he'd keep us out of war." "How can you talk about a good God who lets a train get wrecked? A decent man wouldn't be that cruel."

To such questions one parent may say, "We just don't understand the will of God. Sometimes the things he allows or decrees seem cruel, and yet we have to believe that God is good and sends what is best in the long run."

But another parent sees God's will in a different light.

Karl, at sixteen, is more sensitive than most boys to the misery of the world. Pain has given him acute awareness of the place of suffering in human life. One day, driving along the river which skirts the miserable, crowded huts of "the flats," he remarks to his mother bitterly, "I have no use for a God who allows such things to exist. If he is God at all, he could do something about it. He could allow a fair chance to everybody instead of sending poverty and misery to some."

"I don't think it's God who sends the misery," his mother answers. "Misery and pain are here as a part of this growing, perfecting universe. God struggles against them, or through them, just as really as you or I do. He works in the world for its ultimate perfection. But having given us free will, he can't accomplish his end all at once."

"Then he isn't an all-powerful, infinite being," says Karl promptly. "He's limited."

"In a way he is limited," his mother agrees, bringing the car to a stop on a shaded boulevard where she can talk without dividing her attention. "There are some things he can't accomplish by divine fiat unless he entirely discards the growth of human personality. He has to wait for men to see and understand their responsibility for one another. He has to wait for the slow process of trial and error, for the slow evolution of ideals and their even slower application to real-life situations."

Karl runs his hand through his thick dark hair, as he often does when perturbed. "Then it's rather foolish to talk about the omnipotent will of God when he can't carry out his intention because he's blocked by stupid people."

His mother's face brightens. "There's a lot of difference between what God purposes and what he has to do in a given circumstance. In that sense he's not so different from his human children. We have to adjust our will to circumstance all the time. Take the way your father intended for you to go into the timber business with him. That was his aim, his will. He expected you to become his partner and successor, and all the rest of us agreed. You could say it was our will, too, yours and mine."

"I certainly intended it," Karl says, his face darkening.

"But then after your long illness it looked as if that kind of roustabout life would be too rugged for you. And while you were sick you found out that you have a lot of skill in your hands. So you went to work on plastics, and now, in the circumstances, it's your intention — and also your father's present will — for you to be an inventor of new materials."

"If I'm good enough," Karl says cheerfully.

"So you see our original intention, our purposeful will, is changed to the best possible desire under the circumstances. But behind and through our intentional will and our circumstantial will is what you might call our ultimate will — that's for you to become the best possible man, mature in all your relationships."

She smiles up at her son and he smiles back. But he doesn't speak for a time. Then he says, "So you think that poor housing we passed is God's circumstantial will for those people?"

His mother looks disturbed. "It's tragic, isn't it? We know God means his children to have a better chance than that, but he's defeated by the shortsightedness of some of his human children. It throws an awful responsibility on people who have a little inkling that conditions like those aren't his true plan. But do you know, I think his ultimate will is bound to be accomplished. I think his ultimate will is for his children to care as much for each other as for themselves, and that one of these days we'll all grow into an understanding of his will. Then housing like that can't exist."

After a bit Karl comments, "But those people living right now in those Flats may never live to see the day when his purposeful will, as you call it, is manifest on this earth. They'll have to have a lot of opportunity to grow in eternity or some place beside right here and now."

"I suspect so," his mother agrees. "There's no reason to think this lifetime is the only chance we'll ever have. The universe is large and varied and there may be a lot more experience waiting for us."

Skepticism lingers in Karl's voice. "It can be pretty tough on a fellow who's caught in a squeeze play between God's intentional will and man's messing up of circumstances."

His mother nods slowly. "I think one thing Jesus demonstrated was the necessity to demonstrate God's circumstantial will. I don't believe it was God's intentional will that Jesus come to earth to die. I think he meant Jesus to demonstrate the abundant life which utilizes all of the eternal resource to make men whole and good. But evil men stymied that plan, and in the circumstances it became God's will that Jesus should die rather than compromise. I think it was Jesus' acceptance of his father's circumstantial will with a spirit of full co-operation, without any bitterness, that makes it possible for God's ultimate will to triumph. Ultimately mankind will be 'saved.' We'll catch on. We'll grow up to be his true children."

Karl says slowly, "I'll buy that. I must say it makes sense. Only you have to think a long thought about time."

For many a young person trying to find God's will for his own life may become the paramount concern. The young are inclined to think in immediate personal terms and they want to be sure at once. They ask, "Some people think God's will is one thing and other people think it is exactly opposite. So how can I be sure what his will is for me?"

"It's difficult," some parents will admit. "At best we just stumble along, trying, hoping, probably misunderstanding what God is trying to tell us half the time."

Another parent will say, "But we do have some compass points. When we are in doubt about God's will for some particular course of action, we can turn to the Scriptures and see if the thing we are planning seems in line with the best teaching we find there. We can try to imagine what Jesus would do in the same circumstances. We can consult people in whose judgment we have confidence. Then we can be still, and ask God's direction, and wait for an inner assurance. If we do all of these things, we probably come as near to understanding his will as we can reach at our stage of development."

Some parents would add a cautionary word, pointing out that occasionally we have to act on the spur of the moment, before there is time for prolonged consultation through prayer. It is because of such emergencies that the *practice* of prayer matters. Time spent regularly in God's presence is time spent in sensitizing ourselves to his mind, his expectations of us, his way of communicating with us. "Seek ye the Lord while he may be found; call ye upon him while he is near" is sound advice, because when communication is habitual and open and clear, then we are likely to get a response in the instant of need. Without that accustomed companionship we may not get an answer — not because he isn't available but because we aren't available.

In a family in which prayer is customary, children turn readily for God's help when someone they love is ill. But if the illness does not appear to respond, then their questions fly. "Why doesn't God make Mummy well? He could do it if he wanted to." "Why don't we pray day and night so that God's got his mind on Jimmy all the time?" "Walter prayed and his father got well, but I pray and my father doesn't get any better. I'm just as good as Walter. Why doesn't God hear me, too?" And then

the questions of adolescents, conditioned to the factual
considerations of science. "Doesn't it seem a kind of
superstition to expect a person to be healed by prayer?
After all, in our day medicine knows that some diseases
are incurable." "Isn't it asking God to step outside his
laws to expect incurable cancer to be miraculously
healed?"

Most parents, like most doctors, admit that there are
attested "cures" of diseased conditions for which medicine
offered no hope but which appeared to respond to prayer.
However, few parents, and certainly few physicians,
would attempt to say how or why these exceptional re-
coveries came about. The inexplicable facts remain to
confound our present scientific understanding.

Some parents say simply, "We don't know why some
persons are spiritually healed and others are not so healed
even though they appear to have as deep faith. This is
one of the mysteries of God's ways. He alone knows
why it is important for some to live, and he performs the
miracle."

Others say, with warm finality, "If we could get behind appearances we would probably find that no one
is healed by any strictly spiritual means. Some bodies
are more responsive than others to medical aid or rest or
peace of mind, and they have greater recuperative powers
than anticipated. It will probably be a long time before we
understand all the factors at work, but this is a scientific
world and adequate methods of righting physiological mechanisms will some day be known. In the meantime we
must pay the price of ignorance and partial knowledge.
The point is to go after increased knowledge, rather than
asking God to intervene miraculously."

Still other parents may point out that at least two factors appear relevant to healing. First, it looks as if God's

intent for the body is wholeness, health, for the body is endowed with tremendous power to maintain its own well-being. Its ability to hold salt in the tissues, to maintain blood, to effect an endocrine balance, to distribute oxygen — these and a thousand other incredibly delicate mechanisms are at work all the time to hold on to health and to restore health. A second apparent fact relevant to healing is that mind affects body, that emotional states condition bodily well-being. For instance, the pituitary, master gland of the whole gland industry, manufacturer of a variety of hormones which regulate details of the chemical plant which is the body, not only calls out proper defenses to meet a bacterial invasion or the like, but also responds to an emotional call. An unpleasant emotion such as deep discouragement acts as a stressor just as effectively as threat of freezing or a virus visitation, and the pituitary releases a hormone known as STH which makes us "feel sick." So we say, "sick with discouragement" just as accurately as "sick with a strep throat." Or for the militant emotions agressively expressed, the pituitary has another response; it calls forth its prize constabulary ACTH which, finding no physical aggressors to destroy, can work a multitude of miseries in the system. In some such fashion emotional imbalance produces physical disease.

But the reverse action, so to speak, is just as real. Expansive emotions tend to set the endocrine system in balance. Awareness of God is among the emotional experiences which dissipate worry, fear, resentment, and quicken the hormones which are health stabilizers. In prayer, emotional attitudes may be reset and the heart lifted in joy so intense that the mechanisms of the body are thrown into gear; they begin to mesh. Perhaps in spiritual experience, when perception is heightened and love floods the soul, all of the bodily processes are stimulated so that even the customary time element in healing is foreshortened and what appears an instantaneous regeneration of protoplasm takes place.

Certain thoughtful adolescents will reply that this kind of deduction sounds reasonable but will point out that not all bodies respond to the spirit's quickening by producing physiological health. Why doesn't true spiritual attunement always result in healing? Is God capricious?

To which some parents would answer, "It just could be that even God is bound by his own laws and that he has to work within the limitations of available physiological resources. We know, for instance, that a body is a chemical plant and that it depends upon some sixty-odd nutrients for the material of growth, replenishment and health. But we do not always have access to the proper nourishment. There may come a time when the prolonged lack of some element — whether mineral, enzyme, hormone, vitamin, whatever its name and whatever the cause of its depletion — makes it impossible for the body to maintain, or after long deprivation to recover, its capacity to function. Then medicine cannot set it right, even though the patient has faith. Nor can spiritual aid set it right, even though the one praying has expectancy. If the working material is no longer available, if the body is impoverished beyond the point of setting its necessary machinery in motion again, then restoration of health may be impossible even to God. Whereupon God says, 'Dear child, this physical vehicle of yours is beyond repair. But never mind: it was only your temporary home anyway. Your spiritual body is whole. Come, now, and leave the coarser material for the finer. I am still with you and life is more satisfying as you advance.'"

To such an explanation the insistent adolescent may

again expostulate, "But why? Why should one person be penalized for lack of the basic materials of body-making when perhaps his shortage, his illness, was not his fault?"

This is one of the most difficult questions with which a child can confront a parent who has faith in a moral universe. It requires a longer-than-one-lifetime time sense. A parent has to admit, "It's true that one man's illness may not be his fault in any sense of individual moral responsibility — although we may be more responsible for our own illnesses than we realize. But we are tied into the bundle of life together. We share each other's achievements but also each other's limitations — and this is particularly true of health. For instance, most of us suffer from lack of knowledge of the laws of nutrition, including the relationship between healthy soil, healthy plants, and healthy human beings. Would you say that God 'lets' the ignorant die, then, of diseases caused or complicated by lack of balanced nutrition? I'd say rather that none of us can advance further than some one of us has carved a step and that having given us a universe full of answers, along with inquiring minds and free wills, he cannot always save us from our ignorance."

"But in the meantime, until we smarten up," probes the young inquirer, "a lot of people's prayers for health go unheard."

"Not unheard; not even unanswered. But answered in the only available terms—which may be life on another level of consciousness."

In the field of spiritual healing the next generation may disclose some very cogent answers, for certainly an increasing number of their elders are searching and the quest has a way of passing on to the next generation.

Prayer as an asking is not the only kind of prayer which catches the interest of children. Anyone who has encouraged children to write their own worship services, their own psalms of thanksgiving, their own antiphonies of appreciation for God's goodness, can attest how quick they are to pour out their gratitude and wonder in praise. In private prayer also they are quick to count their blessing and say thank you. It seems sad that as children grow older they praise less often and begin to think of prayer as petition. They tend, like their elders, to focus upon the gift rather than the Giver.

For a child, prayer need not always be expressed in words, but is an experience of companionship. "Today Daddy and God and I went for a walk." "I sat on a big rock with Mummy and watched God make a sunset, and we didn't say a thing, any of us."

Said a five-year-old, "Last night I wasn't afraid because God kept looking in to see how I was doing."

"Did he say anything?"

"Of course not. God doesn't have to talk to tell you things."

Perhaps in prayer, as in other intuitions of life's outreach, a child can lead us.

VIII. What of the Bible?

Hard texts are nuts (I will not call them cheaters),
Whose shells do keep their kernels from the eaters.
Ope then the shells, and you shall have the meat;
They here are brought for you to crack and eat.

JOHN BUNYAN (Pilgrim's Progress)

There was a day, not so long since as the Christian era
is reckoned, when a man was either a believer in the Bible
as the word of God divinely revealed, or an "unbeliever."
The distinction was clear. One came into the fold or remained outside. There was no loitering at the gates, and
children pretty much walked in with their parents. Certainly in those days children were not inclined to ask questions about the authenticity of the written Word of God.
But after some thousand-odd years of practical unanimity
of opinion about the Bible, along came a new light called
"the spirit of scientific inquiry," turning its beams in all
directions and counting no shadows too sacred for its
investigation. It peered into the outer universe and laid
bare the materials of the physical sciences, and then, in
due time, the materials of the biological and social sciences. Man began to feel that he would one day understand his world. So much concern with the universe and
man's place in it did something to the common interpretation of history, including "sacred" history. People
began to ask how and what and why and whence of the
Holy Scripture.

Today there is no "accepted" theory about the Bible

and its place in the affairs of men. There are good men and true who hold to sharply divergent points of view. There is the view which accepts the Bible as divine revelation, different in kind from any other document ever written and peculiarly ordained to be a standard of human conduct. There is also the view which accepts the Bible as a great historical and ethical document, written and compiled by much the same sort of honest and sometimes scholarly men who write great books today, a document which has significance in whatever degree men may find use for it. There is, again, the view which accepts the Bible as one of the outgrown superstitions of the Western world, interesting perhaps for its historical or literary significance but no longer relevant to modern life. Some parents know exactly which view they hold and consequently they know how they will answer their children's questions. Other parents have a degree of sympathy for all three attitudes, and are not exactly sure what they themselves think about the Bible, and still less sure what they should say to their children.

If difference of belief were more sharply reflected in conduct, it would be easier to advise a new generation, "By all odds, *this* interpretation seems to make better men." But to date people of all degrees of goodness seem to be found in all groups. An average child leading a busy life of school and play will run into many of the varieties of conduct and many of the varieties of belief about the Bible. To him there may not seem to be much relationship between the conduct and the beliefs. He will ask questions about all of them, the slant and tone of his questions depending upon his family experiences. Naturally his parents will answer the questions about the Bible in terms of their own understanding of it.

"Do you believe things are true just because they are

written in the Bible?" Dorothy, aged ten, has seldom taken any authority unquestioningly.

"No, I don't," says her mother promptly. "But I think they are written in the Bible because they are true."

"What's the difference?" asks Dorothy, squinting her eyes together as she does whenever she feels a good answer coming her way.

"It's the difference between my telling you that if I catch you cheating you will be severely punished and my telling you that I've found out through years of rather difficult living that it simply does not pay to try to cheat. Knowing me as you do, you probably have some respect for my conclusion."

Dorothy catches on. "You mean that some things are so true that somebody decided they were important enough to write down in a book, and the book is important because what it says is so true."

Her mother laughs. "That's about it. In generations of living together, men found out certain basic things about life: justice *is* more important than might; it *is* harder to keep the tongue than to take a city; loving one's neighbor *is* vastly more effective than tithing of mint and anise. Fathers who had experienced these 'truths' told them to their sons who told them to *their* sons."

"Until finally someone wrote them down."

"That's it, I suppose. And in passing on these true things, parents also passed on the stories about the great men who had discovered them. Sometimes they also passed on legends and parables which made the point of their experiences more plain. Large or small, only important things are treasured from one generation to the next. Gradually these truths which we sometimes call race experience were written down. Finally they were collected into a library of sixty-six volumes which were later put together in one large volume called the Bible."

"I think that does make them more important than if God just sat on a cloud and said them off," says Dorothy comfortably.

"Maybe it's about the same thing in the end," her mother suggests. "The kind of God who is a father to his children would admonish them only for their own good. He'd tell them the things they are bound to find true."

"You mean the way you tell me I'll be sorry if I'm selfish about the playhouse?" Dorothy is always willing to take a lesson home.

Her mother smiles. "I mean the way we all try to save other people from making mistakes which will cost them grief and trouble. Whether you think of the Bible as a sort of great letter from God to his children or as a bundle of letters from our ancestors to us, the book is full of things which people have found to be true. No matter who said them first, man or God, they probably wouldn't have lasted so long if they didn't stand the test of people's living by them."

"It's kind of an important book," Dorothy decides.

"That's what a good many people have concluded."

Lucilla and Maud are next-door neighbors and have been playmates from babyhood. Both are twelve, both are in the eighth grade, both are Girl Scouts, and both go to the same Sunday school in a church which is neither conspicuously conservative nor strikingly radical. In fact, the church, like the town, could be duplicated for friendliness and contentment in many parts of this country. Lucilla's father is a lawyer who knows the troubles of half the town. Maud's father is a hardware merchant by trade and an ornithologist by avocation. Both fathers pay their taxes, vote thoughtfully at each election, and do their bit for better roads, better schools, better sanitation. Both have been church school teachers.

One Sunday Lucilla comes home from Sunday school and goes at once to her father who is picking peonies in the garden. "Father, listen! Do you know what our new teacher, Miss Snyder, said today at Sunday school? She said she thought that the men who wrote the books of the Bible sometimes were just as likely to be mistaken in what they thought as the men who write histories of the United States. She said in an age when everyone believed in miracles, it was just natural for the disciples to believe that Jesus performed miracles when he had such a wonderful effect on sick people. And she said that the story about Jonah and the whale was never meant to be taken as fact. It was a story told to make a point, just like a fable makes a point without having to be a true story at all." Lucilla stops for a breath but her silence shouts, "Now what do you think of that?" And her father answers the unspoken question.

"I'll tell you what I think, Lucilla. I think that the Bible is the word of God, different from anything else that was ever written. I think the Almighty decided what should go into his Book. Many other deeds were done by the Israelites than those which were recorded in such books as Exodus and Kings, but God directed the recording of only such events as he thought would have meaning for people who came after. In the same way, when he reports a miracle, I believe that it was a miracle which occurred just as the story tells it."

Lucilla slips into a garden chair. "But, father, Miss Snyder says that the Bible went through a lot of translations before it ever got into English. She says that there is bound to be human error in any translation, and that the original stories of things like the tower of Babel or feeding the five thousand may have been quite a bit different from the stories we know now."

"The Bible has gone through a great many translations," her father agrees. "Most of the Old Testament was probably first written in Hebrew. Some of the New Testament was certainly handed down in Aramaic and then translated into Greek and later into Latin and then into English. But I believe that God cared enough about his Word to have a hand in all of those translations. I believe that he moved in the minds of the translators, that he called the best men for the task and then guided their hands so that they were able to use the exact word and even the exact punctuation which best suited his purposes. It seems to me not too much to expect of a God who could create the world, the sun and moon and planets, of a God who could make man in his own likeness, that he might also be able to supervise the rendering of his Word."

Lucilla looks at her father with admiration. She decides that he is a good deal like one of the prophets himself; he and God seem to understand each other, both about helping people and about the Bible. "It seems too bad for Miss Snyder to be so mistaken," she says sympathetically.

Maud likewise finds her father in the garden but all she can see of him is his feet protruding from under a blue spruce whose lower branches rest upon the ground. She judges from the feet that some place under that tree is the rest of her father and that he must have located the nest for which he has been looking these many days.

Finally he emerges, dishevelled but triumphant, and Maud begins eagerly, "Listen, Father, you know quite a bit about the Bible, don't you?"

"Well, I've read it," her father admits, as he makes an entry in his notebook. "I've read it between its own covers and I've read pieces of it, in one form or another, in most of the volumes we call English literature. What's the matter with the Bible now?"

"This is no time to be funny, Father. We had a dreadful time at Sunday school."

"About the Bible?" They walk toward the side veranda.

Maud nods excitedly. "Everybody in our grade is supposed to learn the books of the Bible, but instead of drilling us on the names, Miss Snyder told us about how the Bible was put together. You see the thirty-nine books of the Old Testament weren't all written at the same time. And Genesis didn't come first! At least that's what she said. Genesis was one of the last books gathered up out of folklore, but when they went to make the Bible —"

"Just who is 'they'?" Her father stretches out on the porch swing and motions his animated young daughter to a chair. "I wonder now if you mean the seventy scholars who were appointed to gather up the various versions of the various sacred books and decide which should be include in the official Jewish scriptures?"

"I don't know exactly who did it. Do you?"

Whereupon her father launches into the story of the development of the canon, that body of scripture which the church finally accepted, after prolonged argument and many conferences, as the inspired word of God.

"My! I wonder if Miss Snyder knows all that," says Maud admiringly. "You wouldn't think so much work had gone into the Bible, would you? I thought God had just sort of dictated it to somebody a long time ago."

" I think we could say that human experience dictated the books of the Bible. The writers of the books of history wrote from the point of view of Hebrews who were only partially aware that they were forging a nation out of scattered tribes, and less aware that a social process was at work in raising their ethical standards as they struggled against their foes within and without. The compilers of the books of poetry brought together the poems which best reflected the national mood and the longing of human beings who had been through great tribulation. The stories of the heroes — Moses, Joseph, Joshua, Ruth, Samuel, David, and all the others — probably grew as they were told by father to son for generations, but the heroes themselves were real enough. Altogether the Old Testament is probably one of the greatest collections of human experience, and interpretations of experience, ever written in the world."

In her usual fashion, Maud has two questions for every explanation her father makes so that it is dinnertime before her curiosity is satisfied. After dinner she goes to Lucilla's house, according to their Sunday custom. After they have settled the urgent matter of whether they shall first take a walk or read the next installment of a continued story, Lucilla says, "Did you tell your father about Miss Snyder and the Bible?"

"I should say so," Maud admits. "Wasn't it exciting? He knew all about how the books got written and about the Seventy and everything. You know, I felt entirely different about the Bible after he told me all those things, didn't you? I felt that it was kind of important."

"Important? Why I should hope it's important. It's the very word of God. My father said —"

Whereupon the two girls compare stories, first with considerable asperity because each feels that she must de-

fend her father's authority, then with growing concilia-
tion. Finally Maud suggests, "Maybe it isn't so important
how you think about the Bible just so long you get good
out of reading it."

But Lucillia looks doubtfully toward the porch where
her mother is reading. "I wouldn't exactly say it doesn't
matter. My mother thinks it matters so much that Miss
Snyder ought to be asked to quit teaching a Sunday school
class. But of course the important thing probably is
whether the Bible helps you to be good or not."

As the weeks go by and Miss Snyder does not give up
the Sunday school class, the home conversations become
more animated.

"How do you suppose they ever happened to collect all
of Paul's letters to the churches?" Lucilla asks her father
one day.

"It was part of God's purpose that they should not be
lost," he answers firmly. "So when it was time to gather
together the books of the New Testament, these letters
came forth from their various hiding places."

Maud asks the same question.

"I suppose we'll never know just how many letters Paul
did write." her father answers. "No doubt some of them
were destroyed or lost by people or churches who never
thought of their being specially important. But it seems
to me that the most likely theory of their collection is
that when the dramatic story of Luke-Acts was written
some time toward the end of the first century, the Christians were suddenly aware, as they began to read it, what
a tremendous figure Paul was, and what a large part he
had had in the spread of the gospel. So they hunted out
their letters from him and began to read them again and
to exchange copies. Probably these sets of copies of Paul's
letters were treasured in many places before there was any

thought of gathering together the books about Jesus into a canon."

Another day the girls come home with the inevitable question, "Why are there differences in the way Matthew, Mark, Luke and John tell the same stories about Jesus? They can't all be right."

"Oh, yes, they can," says Lucilla's father. "Moreover, they may not be exactly the same stories but different incidents which were much alike. At any rate, God doesn't contradict himself. If there's a difficult statement in the Bible, you can rest assured it is there for a purpose."

Maud's father says, "Use your common sense. Did you ever try to get the story of an automobile accident from a dozen different witnesses? Or the description of a wedding? Or the report of a lecture? Send a lawyer and a doctor and a teacher and a milliner to the same county fair or the same play or the same riot and each will come home with a different tale because he saw the event through his own experience and training. Each of them tells the truth as he saw it."

The questions pile up. "Father, did you know that a part of the New Testament was originally written in Greek and part in Hebrew?" "Why were the apocryphal books first included in the canon and later excluded from the Protestant version?" "How did the Western and Eastern texts come to differ?" "Did you know that for hundreds of years all the Bibles were written in Latin and that everybody had forgotten how to read Greek until scholars like Grotius and Erasmus dug out the Greek language and tried to find old, old copies of the Bible which were written in Greek?"

From Maud's father come the exciting stories of the guarding of the Vaticanus, one of the oldest Greek manuscripts in the world, at the Vatican; and then the finding of another ancient parchment manuscript, in an old abbey on Mount Sinai, by a German scholar named Tischendorf; the rush of scholars to consult this new-old manuscript for its rendering of doubtful passages; its sale to England and its later comparison with the famous Vatican manuscript; the consequent revisions of the "accepted" text. From Maud's father, too, an account of the finding of the Dead Sea scrolls in 1947 by a Bedouin boy who was minding goats on a cliff when he threw a stone into a cave and it happened to hit a jar he never knew was there; whereupon, hearing a sound of something breaking, he went into the cave, looked into the clay jar and discovered in it, and in other jars like it, linen-and-wax wrapped scrolls. Eventually these scrolls were sold to collectors and are still being examined by distinguished scholars of ancient languages, many of whom feel that their contents will add immeasurable understanding to the teaching of the New Testament, as well as to the times in which Jesus lived.

In answer to their constant questions Maud's father also tells the story of the way the Bible was divided into verses for convenience' sake, as late as the sixteenth century, by an energetic publisher who marked them off as he jogged along on horseback on his way to the printer. And the story of Tyndale, the sixteenth century Englishman who demanded that the New Testament be translated into English so that the common man who knew no Latin might have access to its teachings; of Tyndale's consequent imprisonment in Holland where he continued his translations by candlelight in his dungeon until he was brought forth to be burned at the stake. Maud's favorite is the story about the Bishops' Bonfire which was supposed to deliver England forever from all English translations of the Bible, when in reality the burning only made the people more eager to read the English Bible so that more copies were sold and, unknown to the bishops, the money from the sale of these Bibles was being sent over to Holland so that more and better English Bibles might be printed. There seems no end to these tales which Maud begins to call "Bible stories about the Bible." She likes to hear about the Great Bible, a copy of which was chained to the pulpit in each parish church. And she likes to hear about the present-day translations, in preparation for which great scholars are able to use papyrus fragments in colloquial Greek, photostatic copies of old Greek uncial texts, and a wealth of other relevant data never before available.

But if Maud's father furnishes the most exciting tales about the Bible, it is Lucilla's lawyer-father who comes to the Sunday school and talks about the meaning of some of the passages in the Bible. When he talks he leaves no doubt in the children's minds as to what it means to be a Pharisee and pass by on the other side of the road when someone is in trouble. In fact, it seems to Maud as if Lucilla's father could almost have written the New Testament himself because he understands it so well. She tries to explain her feeling to Lucilla one day: "Nobody makes me feel the way your father makes me feel about — about its being important how we live and terribly important how other people get a chance to live, too."

Probably, as the years go by, it will matter less and less to Lucilla and Maud whose father taught which, and they may forget the names of the other pupils in Miss Snyder's Sunday school class, but there will remain a heritage of understanding and conviction without which they both might have been the poorer. With the Bible, as with other matters of religious significance, it is the actual sharing of knowledge and experience which matters —

sharing of experience plus the grace to understand that in the end the child must do his own experiencing.

Of course, many children never have access to the Bible, or are delayed in learning to know it, because their parents have so long considered it an outgrown volume full of odd moral teachings, that it never occurs to them to read it for its dramatic human tales nor to come freshly to its ethical perceptions. Sometimes it takes the child to discover the book to his parents.

Warren is a gangling fourteen when he goes off to prep school. His letters home come regularly enough but are exceedingly sketchy on the subject of his studies. The only teacher he comments on is a "Prof" Harney. "Boy, is he an interesting teacher!" says one letter.

At Thanksgiving time, Warren comes home, more gangling, more enthusiastic than ever. After making the rounds of the house, garage, and refrigerator, he opens his suitcase of books in the middle of the living-room floor. His algebra goes under the davenport in one scoot. "Don't know why I brought it because it doesn't give me any trouble." *Nineteenth Century Poets* goes onto the table with a sigh. "The man who wrote that book's a dope and don't you forget it. Names, places, dates, and poems; lot of tripe." American history, general science, first year Latin, all have their pedigrees read aloud. Then with a flourish, out comes a bright red book which Warren promptly designates as "Prof Harney's book, and say, does he know his way around!" Warren's father reaches for the book. *The Bible: An American Translation.*

"Here, I'll read you a piece," says Warren, taking the book from his father and flipping it open to a well-marked page. Then, long legs apart and red head thrown back, he reads aloud the thirteenth chapter of First Corinthians.

Somehow, his father thinks, the words coming from the

boy sound awfully . . . impressive. He isn't sure whose words they are; sayings of Jesus, probably. Love! that's what he hasn't been showing much of in his life. He's always given Warren a lot, and sent him to the best schools, and paid his way back and forth for vacations. But love. . . that was different. He feels a wave of regret sweep over him. "When I became a man I put away childish things." Maybe he's put away the wrong things. When Warren comes to the end all his father says is, "Fine! You read very well." It is the first man-to-man comment he ever made to his son.

Warren flushes, hoping he has sounded something like Prof. Harney. "Some time I'll read you the fortieth of Isaiah," he offers. "And the hundred-and-third Psalm. Some time I'll read you the whole book of Job."

When he does, his father thinks, he intends to have something to say beside "Fine!"

That night after the boy is in bed, his father goes back to the living room for the red-covered volume. He takes it to bed with him. The margin is full of notes in Warren's almost illegible script. "Blessed are the meek," reads the text, and in the margin is a note, "He means the teachable." "Blessed are the pure in heart" — and in the margin "Single-minded; one purpose; don't clutter up your mind." His father closes the book and turns off the light. But he keeps thinking, and turns the light on again. He remembers his grandmother's telling him the story of Samuel. When he turns the light off for good, it is very late. What a strangely moving book this is. A book about life.

Almost any parent, no matter how he feels about the relevance of the Bible to an adolescent's life, will recognize that the significant aspect of Warren's experience is the fact that someone who had firsthand appreciation of the Bible had introduced the book to the boy. Talk *about* the Bible, like scholarship in the field, can be illuminating, but it is the content which changes lives. In time of stress people do not discuss the authorship of the Twenty-third Psalm; they quote the Psalm. When death enters a family, no one talks about the date and eschatology of the Gospel of John; they repeat the words beginning, "In my father's house are many mansions. . ." When the heart overflows with joy, the words themselves well up, "Bless the Lord, O my soul, and all that is within me, bless his holy name." If all the Bibles in the world were burned tomorrow, it would not be the critics who reproduced the text, helpful though they would be. The text would rise from thousands of ordinary people in whose hearts the words live. And this is a fact of great relevance for parents.

Many parents feel that the Bible is definitely not children's fare; some of the history is bloodthirsty, some of the stories crude, some of the teaching outmoded. And so, knowledgable specialists extract and compile a children's Bible, tempering the blasts to the psychologically protected lambs. Others allow the lambs to browse at will. Either way, the shepherd — who is usually a parent — is the important figure. A good shepherd leads his lambs to the pastures he knows to be nourishing.

The imagination of some children is captured by the tales of the Bible's translation into all the world's languages. "Who translated it into Chinese?" The answer is a saga of determination, loneliness, triumphant lovingkindness. "Who took the Bible into Japan?" One answer is the story of a Japanese official, at the time when the harbor of Nagasaki was a concession of the Dutch, who found a copy of the Bible in Dutch floating in the bay and risked his life by sending a man to China to procure a Chinese version which he could read. Once children start ferreting out the romantic and often breath-taking tales of the spread of the Bible from country to country and tribe to tribe, they may lead their parents upon a voyage of discovery. Some of a child's most barbed questions may come in the form of "Didn't you ever know that..." Of course there are also parents who can head this kind of expedition themselves.

Some children become interested in other scriptures outside the Judeo-Christian tradition. They may read a magazine article or pick up a book of photographs depicting the temples, art, ceremonies, of other religious; they may study in school about the founders of other religions, men who have helped to set mankind's standards high, provided the ethical compulsions by which millions live, influenced cultures older than their own. Often exchange students at high school level bring the concerns of Islam, of Zen, of the Bahais and others into everyday experience. Delegates to the United Nations bring many religious views, traditions, hopes into our shared life. Fortunately in these days parents can find direct answers to questions about the origin and content of other religions in excellent translations of the world's great religious books, many of them available in inexpensive paper-covered editions.

It may come as an amazement to parents to find a teenager approaching his own religion through the side door of appreciating another scripture than his own, a book which familiarity has not dulled for him. A young person familiar with the Gospel of John is likely to be struck by the opening of the *Tao Têh King*, scripture of the Taoists or followers of Lao-tze, "The Way is beyond the power of words to define"; and to see with what subtle wisdom this smallest of all the great scriptures — only five thousand words — makes plain the way of nonviolence.

A high school student is likely to be impressed by the practicality of some of the sayings of Confucius:

"The Superior Man is like an archer who, when he

misses the center of the target, turns and looks within himself for the cause of his failure."

"The Master said, 'By nature men are nearly alike; by practice they get far apart.' "
And surprised to find in the Koran many of the familiar stories of the Old Testament, as well as supreme adoration of the One God, akin to the Jewish insight.

> Say, He is God alone:
> God the eternal!
> He begetteth not, and He is not begotten,
> And there is none like unto Him.

And to find the Koran testifying,

> The sun and moon have each their times,
>   And the plants and trees bend in adoration.
> And the heaven, he hath reared it on high,
>   And hath appointed the balance . . .
> And the earth, he hath prepared it for the living tribes:
> Therein are fruits, and the palms with sheathed clusters,
>   And the grain with its husk, and the fragrant plants . . .
> He created man of clay like that of the potter.

And to discover in the Zend Avesta, Bible and prayer book of the Parsees, or followers of Zoroaster:

> Thou, O Mazda, in the beginning hath formed our beings and consciences and intelligence through Thine own mind. Thou madest life clothed with a body. Thou gavest us the works and words whereby one may freely express his belief. Saith the Lord:

> I created the stars, the moon, the sun, birds and animals.
> But better and greater than all, I created
> The righteous man who has truly received from Me
> The praise of righteousness in the good way.

So like the Masoretic text of Genesis:

In the beginning God created the heaven and the earth: . . .
And God created man in his own image, in the image of God
created he him; male and female created he them; And God
blessed them. . . .

And to read of Buddha's search for enlightenment, of his
tremendous discovery that God has shared his very nature
with the sons of men, of his gathering of his disciples and
their service throughout the rest of his long life. And to
learn the ageless stories of the Hindu scriptures: such a
story as that of the Prince who, after a long and just rule,
finally crossed the desert to the very foot of the mountain
of the gods, to have Indra himself, lord of them all, sweep
down in his chariot prepared to take him to the eternal
mount, only to have the Prince refuse because his hound
dog, faithful through hardship, could not approach the
mighty god—and Indra's final encomium, "Thou hast been
faithful to the meanest of the creatures; enter thou into
thy heritage."

As some parents know, knowledge and appreciation of
other scriptures can greatly illuminate and enliven interest
in the Judeo-Christian scripture. Adolescents are often
struck by certain similarities in story, psalm, and teaching
found in portions of various of the great scriptures; but
also through comparison they may come to far keener
discernment of the central teaching of their own Bible.

But here again with all of these immortal books, parent
and teacher can pass on only what they themselves know
and there is always a chance, of course, that having given
the child the best a parent knows, the child may choose
a different interpretation, which in effect makes a different Bible. This is a hazard — whether hopeful or dis-
couraging — of the shared quest.

IX. What of the Church?

My wife could not help wishing we had some place like a church for the worship of the Sabbath, till I said to her, "There is no place in the world that may not serve for a church, because we may entertain pious sentiments everywhere, and this majestic arch of Heaven, the immediate work of the Almighty, ought more effectually to raise the soul and touch the heart, than an edifice of stone made by the hand of man."

JOHANN D. WYSS (*Swiss Family Robinson*)

"Mother, do I have to go to church today?" "Why does our family go to church, Dad, when Ted's family never does?" "Do you think that going to church is so awfully important if a person feels he can live just as good a life without going?" "Church is kind of an outgrown idea, don't you think?" "Don't you think that doing good is more important than going to church?" "I don't want to join a church, Mother, because I can't live up to all that. Isn't it better to do the best you can without joining anything?"

These are among the questions which parents have to answer. To be sure, there are still communities in which practically everyone who "is anyone" goes to church and asks no questions. Sometimes these communities are Protestant, sometimes Roman Catholic. There are more of them in the south than in the north. In such places children are likely to go to church without much comment, at least until they go away to school. But most American communities, in these days, are pretty well divided as to churchgoers and nonchurchgoers. If one were forced to a generalization he would probably be safe in saying that there are far more highly intelligent, cultured, socially significant (meaning useful to society) persons outside the church than was the case two generations ago. Some critical commentators on the current scene hold that the church is going through one of its periodic cultural lags, that there are fewer great preachers, fewer prophet-priests, less genuine ministration to spiritual need than in any other period since our country began. Others hold that there has never been a day since our nation became a republic when the church — both Catholic and Protestant — has been so aware of its task, so resourceful in making the whole of life the concern of religion. The difference of opinion is itself a commentary on the place of the church in modern society.

Parents are bound to answer questions about the church from the vantage point of their own relationship to the church. Some believe in the church in the abstract without getting around to participate in the particular. Some doubt the relevancy of the church in a modern world but still, for reasons emotional or expedient, continue to give it support. Some out-and-out wish their children spared participation in an anachronism. And at the other extreme, some give complete allegiance to whatever denomination or persuasion of the Church Universal they believe to be "the true church." Those who accept authority themselves are likely to answer their children with authority; either Roman Catholic or Protestant authority.

"Mother, our church is prob'ly the best church in the world, isn't it?" asks eight-year-old Ann, fresh from a heated argument with her chum who goes to a different church.

"We think it is, dear," her mother answers complacently. "From the time of Daniel our message and its interpretation has been foretold."

Ann's expression betrays surprised delight. She didn't know that "we" were as important as that. What she had in mind was the fact that the particular church she attends has the loudest singing in town and the highest steeple. If she was previously sure that her church was the one and only, she is now doubly assured. Unfortunately her small chum is also being assured by her parent, but in a different direction.

Final pronouncements may be a great satisfaction to a child, conducive to security, until he runs into contradictory finalities some of which may seem more reasonable to him than do his inherited finalities. In some communities a churchgoing child with any curiosity or judgment (and most children have both) will find himself confused by the variance of the last word. "The Sabbath means Saturday and that's the day God meant people to worship." "The Sabbath used to mean Saturday but after Jesus' death the early Christians gathered to celebrate his resurrection on the first day of the week, and the word Sabbath was merely carried over to indicate the day of worship." "Jesus practiced immersion and no other form of baptism is scriptural." "Jesus meant baptism to be a symbol for the washing away of one's sins; the important thing is the cleansing of the heart." "Symbols are extremely valuable as aids to worship, reminders of meaningful experience." "Symbols are crutches; a true Christian has no need of them if he worships in spirit and in truth." "Of course deacons, elders, and bishops are necessary for church administration; they are spoken of in the New Testament." "Of course the form of church government makes no difference. Whatever form conserves time, energy, and money and remains pliant is a 'right' government in a given situation." "A church member should be known by certain practices, such as not eating meat on Friday, attending communion, making strict observance of the holy days." "A church member should be known by a way of life marked by love, forgiveness, and integrity."

And so down one road and up another, thousands of parents with the word once for all delivered to the saints. And those who speak the final word seldom see anything funny about there being so many final words, all different. One thing is certain, though: children who question the promulgators of the final word do not get the kind of equivocal answers the rest of us give. And mighty small necessity is laid upon them to exercise their judgment.

It would be comforting to think that most of the rest of us, belonging to neither group of extremists, thoughtfully appraise the church — its nature, ideals, place in society, practical functioning — and reach a considered opinion as to how we can best co-operate with its aims and program, answering our children's questions in line with our adult attitude and action. Usually, however, we do nothing so consistent. We never really come to a conclusion either about the essential nature of the church or its place in the social order, and so naturally our conduct in relationship to it has no core of stability. If our children were sure to ask their questions in words and to insist upon reasonable answers, we might be pushed to a point of view and hence to some consistency of action. But many of our children's questions never quite come to the surface, so they never come to grips with central issues.

Willy-Nilly we continue to answer by example, but having drifted into our position as examplars we seldom offer anything as strong as a conviction expressed in a way of life.

Perhaps one accepted generality about our relationship to the church is that if we have always been lively church members the chances are that we will continue so, especially if our environment is permanent. But a change of environment, a move to another locality, and a new set of friends leaves us open for a changed attitude. Lacking convictions, we are then at the mercy of community forces. And so as our children, who make the change in locale with us, ask questions about going to church or not going, our own uncertainty becomes their answer. And at the same time our uncertainty becomes our question addressed to the church itself.

For instance, the Sherman family were regular church attendants in their home town of Austin. Both parents had been brought up in Sunday School, so to speak; had courted in the young people's organization, and after marriage had continued their interest in the church, with Mrs. Sherman holding offices in the women's society and Mr. Sherman once serving as an usher. Their children's lives also included Sunday School, and semi-regular attendance at the morning service. Then the family moved to a different part of the state and bought a home in the suburb of a sizeable city. The third Sunday after their move they attended the nearest church of their own denomination, but the minister was what John, the fifteen-year-old Sherman, called "a monotonous monologist." John's father pointed out the good aspects of the service but had too much common sense to insist that the hour and a half had been well spent. And so the family cheerfully went from church to church, quite frank to admit to such callers as asked, that they were looking for the place where they felt most at home. Now the rounds have been made.

"If you ask me," volunteers John, since no one has asked him, "not a minister said a thing worth staying awake for except a couple of good illustrations that white-haired man used, and he talked the rest of his forty minutes about nothing."

"If you ask me," says Helen, two years younger, "I was bored all the time. The music was good at the brick church, but we can get just as good music or better by turning on the radio."

"If you ask me," offers Charles, a contemplative nine-year-old, "I'd rather read a book."

Father clears his throat. He knows he ought to make some kind of defense of the churches. He begins cheerfully: "I think there are two or three churches in this town which are really as good as our own church back in Austin, only we are used to that church and we aren't used to any of these churches." As soon as the remark is made, he feels that it might be considered a little weak.

John thinks so, too. "Then I'd say it's a good thing we moved. If we've been spending our time listening to this same kind of palaver and didn't know it, it's lucky we came away."

Feeling the argument slipping, Mother now wades out with an anchor. She is more than cheerful; she is brightly animated as befits this crucial matter. "I do feel that we should support the church. Your father's people have always supported the church and I'm sure mine have, too. If we put our minds to it, we can feel worshipful in any church."

Her remark is met with silence.

At last John speaks, slowly. "Maybe *you* feel worshipful, Mother, but *I* don't. I don't feel uplifted; I don't feel like being better. I can't think with all that chatter going on and I can't even sleep."

"Oh, I can think," Helen breaks in. "I never hear a thing the minister says, after I've listened to see if he is going to say anything. I plan out clothes and make up valentine verses and think of all kinds of things just as well as if I were sitting there alone."

"For that we get up and go to church," observes John pessimistically, "when we might as well be home in bed."

Mr. Sherman feels restive. The children seem to have the better of the argument but there is still family custom and his wife's convictions to reckon with. He makes a firm statement. "I wouldn't want to live in a community that had no churches, and a community can't have a church if all the members stay home and send their best wishes."

At the time Mr. Sherman means what he says but the next week he starts playing golf for the first time in his life. Soon he believes in golf with every muscle, and besides he has a duty there, too. A sedentary man has to get exercise when he can. At first his wife chides him about missing church but when he asks her head-on whether a poor sermon does him as much good as exercise in God's out-of-doors, she has no ready answer. Nevertheless he does tell the children they ought to go to Sunday School and for a time they go. Then one morning John asks, "Why? Sundays I'd rather go bird hunting. What do I learn at Sunday School as useful as ornithology?" Nobody seems to know the answer. Helen's Sunday School teacher comes to call and tells Helen the class is being organized as Girl Campers and they will all have badges and merits. But Helen feels she has passed the badge stage; besides it seems she is up late every Saturday night and needs her sleep. Only Charles sees a reason to go to church. He has joined the boys' band and plays a piccolo. Mother likes the all-day sewing but it comes on the same day her club meets and being new in the club she feels she shouldn't keep cutting. Not one of the Sherman family asks what the church really has to offer that other organizations and pastimes cannot offer. And no one in the church suggests an answer to their unasked question.

There is never any open break between the Shermans and the church. They all go to Candlelight Carols at Christmas. And at Easter every Sherman is in the pew. They would be the last to realize that in Austin they had gone to church on momentum, rather than by conviction, and that in their new community they stay away for the best of all reasons: they have no need the church seems to fill. Certainly they never think of themselves as answering negatively the question of the church's validity. And of course by this time the children have quit asking questions about the church, for the parents have answered in the plainest possible terms.

Some parents, having drifted out of the church as the Shermans have done, would nevertheless encourage the children to stay on in Sunday School or participate in the youth activities or go with their friends to the morning service. They say, "We would like to have the children go until they are old enough to decide for themselves whether or not they want to continue." Or perhaps they remark to the minister, "We don't want Nancy and John to grow up to be heathen like their father and mother." Or, "We don't know what to say to Dorothy when she asks about God and life after death and things like that. We hate to say we don't believe anything. It seems to us she ought to go to Sunday School and learn enough to satisfy her until she is older."

At first glance, it seems that these latter parents are not
being fair. Why give the children answers which they
themselves have found invalid? But judgment is not easy.
Sometimes the parents are honestly not sure they have
chosen the wiser part in making no place for the church
in their lives, not quite satisfied that the best they have to
offer is sufficient for the next generation's need. Perhaps,
they feel, there may be deeper springs than they have
drunk from. At least they want their children to loiter
where such springs may rise, even though their own
experiences in churches have not been helpful.

In another kind of home where church attendance is
customary, there is constant appraisal; a kind of inside
stocktaking.

Edwin is a high school senior and a leader in the young
people's group of his church. One night at dinner he presents his problem. "We had a big argument over at
Marian's about churches. Sam said he was through with
churches because nine out of ten churches he'd ever been
in had such sappy ministers. Katy—she's a Catholic, you
know—said she didn't think you could judge the church
by any one congregation or priest or minister because it
was the Church Universal which Jesus had established and
you have to keep the whole thing in mind."

His mother looks up quickly. "I think she's right. I
think the church is one institution in which the whole is
actually greater than the sum of its parts. The best and
most elaborate individual institution in the country, or the
best denomination—if we could be sure which one that is
—couldn't speak *for the church*. At least not to me.
When I say the church I think of the whole of Protestantism."

"The whole of Protestantism?" Grandfather Wainwright's bright blue eyes twinkle as they often do when
he is enjoying some idea all by himself.

"The whole of Protestantism," repeats his daughter firmly.

"I don't think it's very practical to talk about the whole of Protestantism," says Edwin. "After all, in our daily lives we don't deal with the whole of Protestantism. We deal with one individual church, one group of people who worship in one church building."

"Let us thank the fates for that," says his father fervently. His father is treasurer of the church of their choice. "If we had to carry the burdens of the whole church, the church universal as you call it, we'd be paralyzed. One individual congregation is enough to think about."

"Not for me," says Grandfather Wainwright blithely. "Even the whole of Protestantism is too small for me. When I think of the church I think of that vast body of believers who assemble all over the world for common worship, for praise and supplication, for acknowledgement of sin and hope of pardon, for renewal of spirit through sacrament or silence, for dedication to the service of God."

"Why, Grandfather!" says Edwin proudly. "That's a better statement than the creed any day."

"I'm not sure it means such a lot, though, "says Edwin's father. He directs his remarks to his father-in-law, for the two men like to spar—and the family likes to sit in at the sparring. "It seems to me that this body of believers who make up the Church Universal differ in so many ways— so *many* ways— that they really have little in common, except belief in God and perhaps the desire to lead more godly lives."

"But in having that much in common, they have everything," says his wife. "Everything that really matters."

"That's the way it seems to me," says Grandfather Wainwright. "Once you feel this oneness, the differences no longer seem important. They're merely interesting.

They're merely commentaries on human nature which has so many ways of expressing its longings and strivings. It seems to me it's the common bond of trying to draw near to God that makes us one." He turns to his daughter. "Do you know where I got an understanding of this oneness of longing for God? That time we went to Japan. Remember our trip to the Buddha of Kamakura? There it stands beside the sea. One of the largest figures ever cast in bronze, they say." He turns to his grandson. "Once Kamakura was a great city, and once a temple stood over the statue, but about the time Columbus was discovering America a typhoon carried it away. When we were in Kamakura we stood among hundreds of pilgrims —and also we stood in the Presence. The good Book says, 'He hath not left himself without a witness,' and I felt that That One, as the Buddhists call him, was there. I thought of the devotion of the sculptor of that Buddha and of those who had cast the statue—the same sort of devotion that the old masters put into their paintings of Jesus. And I thought—no, I *felt*—devotion, longing, the search for the thing which Buddha called enlightenment and Jesus called the way—*that's* the search which makes mankind all one. I suppose I was having what might be called a religious experience. For a few moments I really sensed the brotherhood of man, and I sensed it so deeply that the insight has never left me. After that I had a different feeling about the institution we call the church. It's part of something larger than itself, old as time, I suppose, more real than any tangible evidence in buildings or images or clergy or ritual."

After Grandfather Wainwright finishes speaking, no one says anything for a moment. Then Edwin speaks out in amazement. "But Grandfather! You're making churches and temples—heathen temples—all seem part of the same thing."

"Maybe I am," admits his grandfather slowly.

"I don't think you can lump them all together," says Edwin's father. "After all, the church was founded on a totally different concept of life from anything that has ever grown out of any other religion. It's built upon a personality. You can't classify churches and temples and mosques all together any more than you can put Buddha and Confucius and Mohammed and Moses and Jesus into the same category."

"Maybe not," says Grandfather Wainwright. "But I don't think they'd mind. They'd probably have a great time comparing notes, comparing insights, and if Jesus had the most light to offer I think the others would be filled with appreciation."

"But while the others were great teachers, Jesus was the very son of God," Edwin's father reminds him. "I'm afraid your theology doesn't hold water, sir."

"Maybe not," Grandfather admits indifferently. "I always try not to climb too far out on a theological limb."

Now Edwin's father looks a little firm. "But theology is enormously important to an understanding of the church. In fact, I doubt if the church has meaning apart from theology. The church was founded by Jesus; you might say that's the first fact of the church's existence. And the second fact is that he gave its oversight to St. Peter whom he called the rock upon which he said he would build the church. St. Peter passed on his high commission to those whom he chose. They in turn ordained others who succeeded them, and so the authority of the church has been passed from priest to priest."

"Priest?" asks Edwin in surprise.

"I'm speaking of the minister in his capacity of priest.
As the successors of St. Peter, the priests speak for Christ
in his church. So I'd say that the church and theology are
rather inseparable considerations."

Edwin looks at his father with admiration; he never
knew his father had such a strong feeling about the
church. Then he sees his mother looking at his father
with bewilderment.

"But, darling—" his mother begins. Edwin knows the
tone. It means she intends to disagree as tactfully as possible but to disagree. "But, darling, the church I grew up
in doesn't believe at all that Jesus founded his church upon
Peter the man. Many people think he founded it upon
Peter's confession—"Thou art the Christ, the Son of the
living God." That's what he meant by the rock. And
they don't think Peter could pass on his authority. They
think only God can give a man spiritual authority. In
fact, maybe no one but God knows who has spiritual
authority. Maybe that's theology, too, in a way, but it's a
different theology, although we're still talking about the
same church."

Grandfather Wainwright chuckles. "You see—here we
have a schism."

Edwin laughs, too. He enjoys seeing grown-ups push
each other into a corner, even when he doesn't know
which corner he chooses for himself. But his father does
not laugh.

"Not a schism, for there can be no splitting of the true
church. The most you could say is that we have different
levels of understanding. But the true church is indivisible
and ecumenical."

"Meaning?" asks Edwin.

His grandfather answers. "From the Greek *oikou-
menikos*, meaning universal, general. It's the big word in

the World Council of Churches, and it's one big word I
go for. For my money, all who try to follow Jesus belong
to him and hence to his church. And as long as people are
trying to follow my Master I feel one with them. So I can
go to church anywhere. I don't give a continental whether
the church happens to be some plain little meetinghouse
which prides itself on its bare and unimaginative interior,
or whether it happens to be a high-vaulted cathedral
which offers every aid of beauty and aesthetic appeal. It
doesn't matter whether the litany is in English or in Latin
or in some tongue I can't understand a word of. I can still
worship and I do."

"Well, that's certainly ecumenical," Edwin's father says,
wishing to keep everything agreeable.

"And I hope not unscriptural," says Grandfather, a
shade complacently.

"On that we might not agree," his son-in-law answers.

Edwin's mother says, "I guess we all believe that the
church is bigger than any of its parts. And we feel a kind
of pride and participation in the Church Universal. But I
must admit that I still like my own church best. I believe
in the tenets of my own denomination; I like our way of
administering the sacraments. I'd go to a good deal of
trouble to find a church which sings the hymns I like to
to sing and uses the ritual I like to follow. Not to mention
feeling it is important for Christians really to be of use in
the world—as our church, it seems to me, tends to make
them."

"I'll buy that, Mother," says Edwin. "Different people
prefer different kinds of houses and yet we all believe in
the home. And we like our education served up differently—in my school the profs spend half their time making sure they're different—and yet we all believe in
education and work for it. I guess it's only natural to like

different ways and methods in churches. But even if I do
like our ways best, still I've got enough sense to know
they're not so awful important."

" 'Awfully important,' " his mother corrects.

" 'Very important,' " says his father. The corrections
are automatic and in no wise detract from the family's
interest in what Edwin has been saying. Nor do the corrections bother him in the least; he doesn't hear them. But
Grandfather begins to chuckle aloud.

"Tell you what," he offers, "I'll take you all to a church
next Sunday where you have to stretch your imagination
to feel at home. It belongs to the Pentecostal Assemblies
of Jesus Christ, one of the Holy Roller group, and the
congregation 'speaks with tongues' when the meeting gets
under way." Grandfather rises from his chair, then stops
short and says seriously: "But before you leave you'll feel
a part of even that group. I think you will. I did. A lot
of people who formerly felt forgotten by the church are
finding something they need right there. It's a wonderful
thing the way this being a part of a group of like-minded
seekers after truth does bring people together. In fact,
it was the urge to share common experience which gave
the church vitality in the first place. People on fire with
a sense of mission for building the Kingdom of Heaven
are bound to meet to make plans, to renew their strength
and devotion, and to worship the one they serve. I tell
you that if the church were wiped off the earth today, by
night people would be gathering together again and out of
their common need and devotion a new movement would
arise, and it would be a new church. That's the way it is!"

Perhaps it is worth noting that in a family such as
Edwin's, where conversation about the church flows
freely, although such discussion may not be frequent, the
interest of the debate comes out of the fact that the family

has had experience with more than one kind of church representing more than one denomination. Without experience in churches with differing emphases, different points of view, how can growing individuals learn to weigh essentials and nonessentials? But once they are emotionally comfortable in a new atmosphere, once they no longer feel the strangeness of a different way of worshiping, their minds are open for entertaining the possibility of different beliefs, for deepened understanding.

The Protestant child's first visit to a Catholic church is likely to bring forth more questions than usual and he is fortunate if his parents can answer his questions with understanding, with historical explanations and genuine appreciation. Understanding and appreciation of their Catholic friends rises in many Protestant homes from happy childhood visits to Catholic churches. Emotional prejudice, habit prejudice, is harder to break down than intellectual prejudice.

In helping the child to become acquainted with forms of worship and tenets of belief other than his own, Protestants will find a rich heritage in the Jewish synagogue. Here again, sinking his roots into the rich soil of generations of religious thinking, the child draws up nutriment for his own religious growth. The prophets of the Old Testament will come to life for him, their impassioned words ringing against a sounding-board of present-day injustice. The ancient "heritage of the godly" belongs to the Christian child as well as to the Jewish child. And when he learns to say, *Shema Yisrael Adonai Elohenu Adonai ehad*—(Hear, O Israel, the Lord our God, the Lord is one") in the very accents of those who pledged their lives by those words perhaps three thousand years ago, he has learned more of the history of religion than he can get from books.

But there is, of course, a point at which one guards against his child's becoming an experience-collector in churches, just as he would guard against the child's insistence upon continually changing grade schools. The church, like the home, is a place for steady growth, for carrying responsibility, for increasing understanding and sympathetic criticism.

One way in which a child deepens his sense of belonging to a church which is larger than the congregation housed in one certain building, is his acquaintanceship with the world-wide work of his denomination. Here, among those who serve for joy of serving where need is fundamental, even elemental, the church's growing edge is often apparent. Here the church has vitality, immediacy, significance. Knowledge about the medical, educational, social, evangelical service of the church on its frontier gives a child a sense of participating in a fellowship not entirely of this world, neither space nor race bound, unfettered by the limitations of culture and time.

To be sure, a child's sense of belonging to, having a part in, the world-wide mission of the church eventually has to grow beyond denominational lines, and does so when parents have an eccumenical outlook. Who cares whether Hall Young of Alaska was a Presbyterian or a Methodist, Isabella Thoburn of Lucknow a Methodist or Disciple of Christ, Alfred Shelton of Tibet a Disciple or Baptist—and so down the roster. How many can name, offhand, the denominational affiliation of David Livingstone or Mary Slessor, of William Carey or Robert Moffat, or Adoniram Judson or John Hunt? Children, being natural hero worshipers, are quick to claim their heritage from the pioneers of the Church Universal.

In our day, one way in which young people develop allegiance to the Church Universal is in the unself-conscious ease with which they move from one denomination to another. The increasing number of "union meetings," of all sorts of young people's groups, increases the possibility that the adolescent may find a church which suits his needs better than the one to which his parents belong. He may have a nature which responds to ritual and feel that the more informal service of his home church has left him cold without his knowing why. Or if he is used to intricate ritual, he may turn to the simple quiet of worship in a Friends' meetinghouse. The preferences for certain forms of worship are more likely to become apparent in the adolescent than in the younger child because the adolescent has a new self-awareness which makes him conscious of his moods. Whatever gives him peace and integration, through the years when so much new emotion is pulling at him, is deeply valuable to him. Moreover, he may develop insight beyond his parents and uncover meaning they may have missed. If so, his parents may have to call forth in themselves a large measure of understanding. For while it makes no difference to some parents to what variety of church their sons and daughters go, other parents feel their children's preference for another church as keenly as if the children had expressed a preference for another home.

"Alan Lee!" says his mother in great distress. "You can't mean that you want to join an Episcopal church. Why we've been Methodists on both sides of the family ever since Wesley. My grandfather and two of your father's uncles were Methodist ministers. You know that."

Of course Alan knows but he feels that it has about as much relation to his present life as the fact that Jefferson was the father of the Democratic party. In the Episcopal church on the corner of Tenth and Harper, he feels that he has found the spirit and the ritual he needs. Maybe he

has also found a gray-eyed girl who carries her prayer
book demurely and enters into the service, kneeling and
rising and kneeling again, with a grace which Alan does
not feel his hearty sisters possess. Maybe in his mind the
girl is mixed up with the question of ritual and Alan
doesn't know it. Whatever the reason, if the new church
meets Alan's needs it is the church for him. In it he may
grow to maturity without disillusionment and find, as the
years add responsibilities, that he has a place for the continual renewal of his spirit. On the other hand, his new
allegiance—like his need—may be temporary and he may
eventually return to the church of his fathers.

Interestingly, a mother who may once have felt that
she could never go back to a half-empty pew in the Baptist
church after John turned Congregationalist and Mary
turned Dutch Reformed, may later find herself quite
happy in the feeling that she has furnished young leader-
ship for sister churches. She can lean back upon the realization that the church exists for the nourishment of human
hearts and for the service of mankind.

Some questions about the church can scarcely be raised
until the child has had experience in the church. For
instance, a discussion of ways to worship has to grow out
of the experience of worship. Awe and adoration come
easily to a child who has not yet learned to explain away
life's wonders. Moreover, most children like to articulate
their feelings and at times like to share whatever they can
articulate. Hence they enter easily into corporate worship. Singing hymns with a churchful of people, old and
young, helps to bring about emotional comprehension of
the very fact being celebrated in worship. "Holy, holy,
holy, Lord God Almighty." "Safely through another
week, Thou has brought us on our way." "Joy to the
world, the Lord has come." "My faith looks up to Thee."

"A mighty fortress is our God." Worship never happens in the past tense nor to someone else. Either the child participates in a vital and immediate experience or he has no very pressing question about worship.

But when he has once experienced corporate worship, then he may be full of questions as to why he cannot always feel worshipful in church, or in all churches; as to what order and form of service brings people nearest to the One he worships. Watching the celebration of certain sacraments, particularly of baptism and holy communion, may raise questions about symbolism in general and particular, about the use of ceremonies in initiation into the living fellowship of the church. Or, a different kind of experience—say, the silent worship and informal testimony of Friends at a First Day meeting—may precipitate a different kind of question about the availability of Inner Light for the direction of each dedicated believer.

At heart, most of us realize that our children's questions about the church are really questions about their life's orientation, toward what and whom, and with how complete a degree of loyalty. For behind the institution stands the personality of Jesus to whom the institution demands allegiance in the form of open commitment to the way of life he taught and demonstrated. As responsible answerers we may decide for or against "belonging" to a church, but we can scarcely ignore either the questions with which the church confronts the child or the questions the child poses to us.

X. What about Babies?

Where did you come from baby dear?
Out of the everywhere into the here.

GEORGE MACDONALD

Anita has been playing with her building blocks, talking to herself in the animated fashion of a four-year-old who is forever acting out stories. This story appears to be about a mother who went to the store and bought two new children. "Where did you get me, Mummy? Where'd I come from?"

Mother, absorbed in letting down the hem of one of Anita's dresses, is taken by surprise. Somehow she had imagined that when the child asked the inevitable question it would arise logically from some such event as their dog's having puppies, instead of popping out of irrelevant play. She looks at Anita for a moment, "Where did you come from?" she repeats. "God sent you, dear." It is a beautiful answer, she thinks to herself, never having grown used to the wonder of having a child. But it does not satisfy Anita.

"How did he send me? In an airplane?"

Mother hesitates. After all, four years is young to try to understand the process of birth, and she doesn't know how much or how little she should explain to the child. There is the stork answer and the answer about the doctor's bag, but it seems to her as if those are lazy answers which lead to further embarrassment. By this time Anita is standing by her mother's knee, drawn by the very fact

that her question is not answered so quickly as usual.
Mother snaps off a basting thread, and turns to the child.

"You grew from a seed, darling. Practically everything
that lives grew from some kind of seed."

"Did I grow in the ground like a radish?" Anita is
incredulous.

"Gracious, no. Different kinds of seeds grow differently. The seeds of plants and trees grow in the ground.
The seeds of chickens and birds are hidden in their eggs
which grow in the mother hen's body. Then when the
hen lays the egg, she has to keep it warm for quite a while
until the little chicken is strong enough to break through
the shell."

Anita smiles delightedly. She has seen baby chickens.
"So you just laid an egg," she says, patting her mother's
hand proudly. "I never knew you could do that."

"Oh, no! Animals don't lay eggs the way chickens do,"
her mother hastens to explain. "Their babies remain inside
the mother until they are big enough to be born alive. So
a mother dog has puppies and a mother cat has kittens. And
human mothers have baby girls and baby boys."

"Hum," comments Anita thoughtfully. "So it's different with all the different kinds of things." And then,
whirling around to her toys, she is absorbed in pretending
that she is a baby again.

Thus it happens that Anita's mother does fairly well
with her little daughter's first questions, but she could
have saved herself that moment's hesitation and her incipi-
ent embarrassment if she had realized that she and Anita
were really talking about different subjects. She was
thinking of sex with all its adult connotations. But Anita
merely wanted to have herself accounted for: how did
she get here?

Most of the questions children ask about origin are just

such questions of mechanics, springing from the same curiosity which makes them ask, "Where does the rain come from? Who starts it?" "How did the world get made?" "How did the stars get in the sky?" If the answers call forth from the child any emotional reaction, it is the emotion of wonder. And the child's world is so full of wonders that he easily makes room for another.

If the parent could remember that the small child's questions are to be taken at face value—no more—then he would find himself emotionally free to give quick, plain, complete answers. The trick is to see the questions in the simple framework of the child's curiosity and to answer them from the point of view of the child's need.

When a very young child asks about his beginning, he is likely to ask only two or three casual questions which, if answered plainly, satisfy his curiosity. If he is satisfied he may forget both his questions and their answers and come back a year or two later to ask the same questions again. Indeed, this questioning process may occur two or three times before the information makes enough impression to remain in his mind.

But not all children, even as young as Anita, are so quickly satisfied as she with their first conversation on the subject. Some will push their questions until the entire process of birth seems plain to them. The most insistent question seems to be, "But if I grew inside of you, Mother, how did I get out?" Sooner or later, that question becomes uppermost and then the answer must be given.

An increasing number of parents turn for help to books written especially for the child. In any one of several excellent books on the subject, pictures help to make the story plain. The book may begin by presenting a black page with a tiny white pin point in the center under which is the caption, "This is how small you were when you began." And then will follow the stories, simply told, of the reproductive processes of plants and animals. There will be a short chapter on the fertilization of seeds, another on the fertilization of the hen's egg and the development of the baby chick. The story of the way in which animals carry their young is likely to have illustrations of a mother cow with her calf, a mother sow feeding her piglets, a mother bunny with her large family. Then comes the story of the human baby, probably with diagrams that show the location of the uterus in the mother's body and the relative size of the baby at different stages in its development.

Usually a young child will not be interested enough to listen to the reading of the whole book at one sitting. He will follow along for some pages and then either wander off to his play or return to his original question, "How was I born?" But his parent can answer, "I want you to know the whole story because it's quite an important story and we will read some more tomorrow."

Naturally it is sometimes easier for the parent when dealing with a young child to sketch the contents of the book in his own words, using the pictures by way of outline and illustration. Naturally, too, different children ask different sorts of questions, and whether the parent reads the story or tells it he has to be ready for interruptions.

One advantage in answering the child's questions with the aid of a book is the fact that the book can be left on his bookshelf for further reference. The child will occasionally pick it up to look at the pictures which are likely, in time, to lead to further questions. Thus between the book and the questions, the parents have a fairly secure feeling that the child is getting information as fast as he needs it.

It is soon after Leonard's seventh birthday that he
climbs up on his mother's bed one morning with the
request he has used since babyhood, "Tell me another
story, won't you?"

"What shall I tell you today?"

"Tell me about when I was born." He snuggles under
the covers ready for a good time.

His mother has told him on other occasions some of the
facts about birth, but for some reason he has not mentioned the subject now for more than a year. Today she
senses that this time he will want more information. She
says, "Downstairs on the third shelf of the bookcase by
the door is a little book called *How You Grew*. You trot
down and get the book."

Leonard goes. He comes back, climbs into bed with
the book and is at once absorbed in the pictures, turning
the pages rapidly.

"Slow down," suggests his mother, "and I will read you
about them." A half-hour passes quickly and she says,
"We will read some more tomorrow."

"Tonight," begs Leonard. "Tonight when I go to bed."

When night comes he appears with the book and his
mother begins to read again. When she comes to the
word "spermatozoon," Leonard halts her. "How many
letters? Let me see that word."

Mother points it out, wondering to herself as the child
spells it aloud over and over whether he has some porno-
graphic tendency she was never aware of. Finally he
exclaims: "Well, sir, that's the longest word we know. It
has twelve letters. Prob'ly it's the longest word in the
dictionary."

His mother smiles as she realizes anew that curiosity
counts everything grist for its mill, and the reading goes
on. Leonard makes matter-of-fact comments now and

then, and appears moderately interested. When the book is finished and Mother sits waiting for additional questions, he merely yawns widely and kisses her good-night. It is a good story finished and that's that.

The next day is Saturday and the two little boys from next door, who are rather new neighbors, arrive to play before Leonard is downstairs. His mother hears him calling over the banister: "Hey Buddie! Walter! Come on up. Do you know how long it takes an elephant to have a baby elephant? Come here and I'll show you a picture of ten little pigs all born at the same time."

A few minutes later Mother goes into Leonard's room and finds all three boys lying on the floor looking at the pictures in the new book. She stops aghast. It is one thing to tell her own child what he wants to know, but it is something different to educate her neighbor's children. From the conversation it is plain that Buddie and Walter know nothing at all on the subject of babies. Indeed they know less than nothing for they have a lot of misinformation.

"It's a funny thing," says Walter, "that my mother didn't know about this."

Buddie's long clear laugh rings out. "She must have been asleep when I was born because she thinks that the doctor brought me in a bag."

"She found me under a bush in the garden," says Walter, turning to Leonard's mother. "Now how did she suppose I got there?"

Mother has an inspiration. "Lots of people make up fairy stories about how their babies came, just the same as they make up jolly tales about the way Santa Claus comes. We all like the Santa Claus stories even when we know they aren't exactly facts."

"But I'm no baby," says Walter. He is disgusted.

"Bless your heart," says Mother, "all of us mothers go right on thinking our children are little kids even when they grow taller than we are."

Mother feels she is doing rather well by her neighbor, but her apprehension is none the less real when she thinks of going next door and having to announce. "Pardon me, but I have just told your offspring the facts of life." She is fond of the mother of Walter and Buddie and most certainly does not want to hurt her.

However, at the moment she cannot take the book away from the children without filling Leonard's mind with a new set of questions. So she does the common-sense thing and sees the incident through, answering the boys' animated questions with offhand explanations as she makes Leonard's bed. By and by, the boys go off to play and Mother goes off to think.

Later in the morning she goes to her neighbor's house. She begins by telling about Leonard's questions, and then edges in the fact that in her experience with Leonard's two older brothers she finally decided it was easiest to tell them the full truth from the beginning. She comes to the place in her recital where she must tell how Buddie and Walter arrived on the scene and were met by Lonard's enthusiastic offer to share his book.

"Oh my goodness!" cries the neighbor. Mentally Mother reaches for the doorknob to escape. But her neighbor is beside her, radiating gratitude. "I'm so grateful! I'm so much obliged! You've no idea how you've helped me. The boys have asked so many embarrassing questions lately, and I've told them so many jumbled answers that I just didn't know what they might come out with in public. I've been hoping that some boy at school might tell Walter the truth and then he'd tell Buddie and they'd keep still."

This is no time for comments on pedagogical procedure. Besides, the mother of Leonard feels that the mother of Buddie and Walter has probably already got the point of anything she might have to say. Instead, she offers to lend the book. The conversation turns to children's books in general. And finally Mother goes home greatly relieved.

But she might not have met with such a cordial reception from her neighbor, for some mothers still believe that ignorance is the best guarantee of virtue and they resent bitterly any attempt on the part of school or mothers' club to impart sex information scientifically. Nevertheless, the best approach to such mothers is probably the indirect one of suggestion through the Parent-Teacher Association or the Women's Club that one of the excellent films on the subject be bought and presented to the school.

Sooner or later almost every child makes more or less the same remarks. "It would take such a big opening for a baby to come through, Mother! I should think that everything inside of you would fall right out too." And then the mother explains the elasticity of muscles which can, when necessary, let the tiniest of openings stretch to considerable size. The child has had some experience through which to understand this explanation because he knows the use of the rectal muscles and realizese that defecation is a normal and usually painless process. It seems reasonable that nature should provide another scheme of the same general sort for letting babies be born.

Most children also comment, "But didn't it hurt awfully to born such a big thing as a baby?"

"Very new babies aren't so awfully big, and their bones are soft. Even the bones of the head are soft enough so that being squeezed a bit doesn't harm the baby at all. Nevertheless it's true that having a baby does hurt a good deal. That's one reason a doctor comes to look after the mother and baby. Sometimes he gives the mother some medicine which makes the pain easier. And the nice thing is that as soon as the baby is born, the pain is all gone. The mother is usually so thrilled over the baby that she forgets all about its hurting her."

Many children, their curiosity satisfied over the mechanics of birth, want the rest of the tale immediately. "Were you glad I was a girl (or a boy)? Was Daddy glad? What did I look like? Did I cry? What did I do first?" It seems important for the child to know all the little things about his becoming *himself* and he will call for that part of the story over and over.

The ideal time to explain to a child the process of a baby's prenatal development is when the family is expecting a new little brother or sister. Then the child feels that something tremendously interesting is happening to *his* family; the baby will be *his* brother or sister; it is *his* mother who is helping the baby to grow. His interest is personal and his healthy curiosity has a logical focus.

Arthur is a rough-and-tumble little boy, unusually fond of babies. No matter how fast he may be dashing down the sidewalk on his roller skates, he comes to a halt by every strange baby carriage and takes a look at the occupant. When he is nine years old his mother tells him that their own family is going to have a new baby. At once he is elated and proprietary. He knows, from earlier conversations, that a baby grows inside its mother until the time comes for it to be born. But he has never had any special interest in the subject before.

"How long will it be before it comes?" he asks.

"Six more months," his mother answers. "It takes nine months for a baby to grow strong enough to be born, and it is now three months since the baby started growing."

"You couldn't hurry it up could you? Eat more or something?"

"Not very well. Nature can't be hurried."

"It doesn't take a rabbit nine months," Arthur observes. "Fred's rabbits can have bunnies in six weeks. Fred's father says that you can just about count on six weeks after the father comes to visit the mother rabbit. He has to borrow a father rabbit from Ernie." Arthur has never questioned the father's place in human procreation, nor does he do so now. He merely adds, "You'd think a person could have babies as quick as a rabbit.."

"The time depends somewhat upon the size of the baby, although not altogether. It takes a mother elephant nearly three years to have a baby elephant."

"But look what she gets! Oh, boy!" Arthur's eyes shine. In a way a baby elephant appeals to him more than a mere brother or sister.

For some days thereafter, Arthur asks questions about the forthcoming baby. He may be playing hilariously and suddenly be reminded of something he wants to know. As happens in regard to his other interests, there seems to be a certain fomenting of ideas deep within him. He speaks when the ideas come bubbling to the surface.

"What does the baby eat? It has to grow. Does it nibble like a fish inside of you?"

Mother, who is writing a letter at the time, takes a sheet of paper and begins to draw a picture. She has drawn so many pictures—of stomachs and livers and hearts and brains and all the things which Arthur calls "the inside works." Arthur likes these impromptu lessons on paper. He stands beside her now, watching with interest. She draws a somewhat pear-shaped figure.

"This is a kind of sack called the uterus," she explains.

"The uterus is an organ a woman always has in her abdomen, although she uses it only when she is going to have a baby. It is the baby's cradle, you might say, because the baby lies snugly inside it for the whole nine months. It is one of the most interesting organs in the body because it can grow many times its ordinary size without hurting the other organs around it, such as the stomach and spleen and liver."

Arthur nods. He knows something about the other organs. "But how can the baby get food? It can't grow on nothing, can it?"

"While the baby is being carried inside the uterus,"— mother uses her pencil again—"the uterus grows a special lining called the placenta. This placenta is filled with little blood vessels not directly connected with blood vessels of the uterus but so near that there is an interchange of tiny substances of nutrition. These particles of food, too small to see, sort of seep from the mother's blood vessels to the baby's blood vessels. The main idea is that the food does get from the mother's uterus to the placenta, and then the placenta is connected to the baby's abdomen by a special cord called the umbilical cord."

"Do you mean a cord like a string? How funny."

"I mean a cord about as big around as your finger and maybe twenty inches long. One end of the cord is fastened to the placenta, as I said, and the other end to the baby's abdomen. Inside the cord are two arteries and a vein to carry the blood back and forth from the placenta to the baby. So you see the baby does have a blood supply of its own, in a way, but still it depends on its mother's body for every single thing which makes it grow —for the minerals for its bones and the food for its muscles and blood."

"Well, I never," is Arthur's old-fashioned exclamation.

He chuckles to himself. "The baby can't get anything to eat different from what you eat. If it wants an ice cream soda, you will have to eat it for him." Then he has another thought. "If the baby is fastened to the placenta by a cord, how can the baby ever get born? Does it break the cord?"

"Nature has a better way than that," his mother explains. "The cord is rather long—almost two feet long —so the baby can be born easily enough, and then the first thing the doctor does is to take a sterile pair of scissors and snip off the cord close to the baby's abdomen. Then a few minutes after the baby is born, the placenta comes out, too, just like a worn-out lining which the uterus doesn't need any more. The doctor disposes of it, cord and all. Then the uterus takes a rest and slowly shrinks to its former size."

"Did all of that happen to me?" Arthur is feeling rather important.

"It certainly did. Just about the same thing happens to every baby. Some day our new baby will grow up and ask questions about the way *it* came to be born."

Some weeks go by before Arthur makes another observation. He is in the living room with his parents after breakfast. His father is reading the paper and his mother is standing before the mirror putting on her hat ready to go shopping.

"I see our baby is growing," he observes. "If it keeps on, you'll have a tummy as big as the milkman's, I guess."

"But more important," comments father.

"Mother's more important than you are," says Arthur suddenly. "A person might think a man's more important because he can lift so much and run engines and be an explorer. But he can't have a baby." He stops. "Or could he, if he wanted to badly enough?"

"No, he couldn't," Father agrees. "That's one place where nature has put the responsibility on the woman."

"Then listen here," says Arthur. "You're really no relation to me at all, are you, Dad? Why should people say I've got your eyes and chin? Everything I've got came from my mother."

In this offhand manner arises the question whose answer will determine much of Arthur's future attitude toward relations between men and women. His father and mother have known that the question might come any day now.

So his father says in a matter-of-fact tone: "What do you mean, your mother gave you everything? She's smart but she isn't that smart. It takes a mother *and* a father to have a baby." Father puts down his paper. "You see, human beings are very much like other animals in the way their bodies work. They all eat and they all digest and assimilate on about the same principle. Likewise they have their young on about the same principle. The mother develops the egg inside her body. But no egg would ever start to grow into a baby unless the father gave it the living germ which makes it grow. The germ is called a sperm or spermatozoon—a long word for a tiny organism too small to see without a microscope. The sperms are developed in the testicles of the father. The testicles are two baglike structures connected with the penis. In a boy, they are small and unimportant because they aren't used. But when a boy becomes a man old enough to be a father, then the testicles grow larger and begin to secrete a fluid called semen. It's a heavier fluid than water and although there is not much of it, it contains a great number of these tiny spermatozoa any one of which can fertilize the egg and make it grow."

"Is that what fertilize means? Make it so it can grow?"

"That's it. The eggs are formed in two little sacks

called ovaries inside the mother's body. About once a month, one of these eggs makes its way into the uterus so that a baby can start to grow there if the egg is fertilized by a sperm. So then, if the mother and father decide they would like to have a baby start to grow, the father must see that the sperm is sent to the egg. The way he gets the sperm to the egg is to insert his penis into the mother's vagina and let the semen from his testicles flow through the penis into the vagina. You remember that the vagina leads right into the uterus. It's really the hallway to the uterus and these tiny sperms, too small to see, swim into the uterus until one of them finds the egg and unites with it. Then the egg starts to grow. So the new baby is literally made by both the father and the mother. Although the spermatozoon is much smaller than the egg—and the egg is scarcely as big as the head of a pin—still it carries half the baby's characteristics. So the baby has just as much chance to look like his father as to look like his mother."

"And so we all get started the same way," says Arthur. "Famous people and poor people and everybody. You'd think—"But he doesn't pursue the subject now. He seems contemplative for a moment, as if about to ask further questions. Then he dives under and comes forth with his catcher's mitt. "Fred told me I'd find the good old mitt right here at home. I thought all the time we'd left it on the field."

Five minutes later he is bounding down the front steps, and his parents hear him shriek, "Hi Fred! Spitzy! Hi! I found the mitt. Lookutit."

Mother looks at Father. "Do you suppose he'll remember all that?"

"Probably not. But he'll remember the general idea. And the next time he has a question, he'll remember that he was interested in what he learned today and he'll come back to ask some more."

"Do you think that maybe we should have said something about just one man and just one woman and all that?"

"I do not," says Father emphatically. "The boy hasn't any experience to comprehend the emotional coloring. Wait until adolescence begins to tug at him. Wait until he knows the difference between girl and girls. I'd like to make a wager that when Arthur grows up he won't be able to remember when or where or from whom he learned the baby lore. It will come out of the storehouse of things he's 'always known' just as he now claims he's always known how his digestion works."

Naturally, Arthur's questions might have gone on for some time and might have turned in any one of a dozen directions. How many sperms does the semen contain? What happens to the ones which do not unite with the egg? Is the semen ready whenever the father needs it? What happens to the egg if no sperm comes to fertilize it? The only sure thing about such questions is that they will reflect curiosity about the mechanics of fertilization and will be as unemotional as questions about a cross-cut saw or an automobile engine—if there is no emotional coloring in the parents' explanation. And, of course, if the child's previous questions have been answered in a straightforward manner.

During the remaining weeks before the baby is born, Arthur's interest is in the mechanics of its development: "What keeps the baby from sticking tight to the placenta?" "Does it lie straight out or curled up?" "Does it turn over?" "If the mother died, would the baby die too?" "How does it finally know when it's time to get born?" All of which are answered as completely as seems necessary for the satisfaction of his own honest curiosity.

Only once does Arthur broach the subject of the baby in the presence of anyone else. One night there is a guest for dinner. Chloe, the maid, is pouring drinking water. Suddenly Arthur speaks up: "Give my mother plenty of water, Chloe, because the baby floats in water. The water sort of cushions it so that if my mother bumped into a door or something, the baby wouldn't get hurt so easy."

No one makes a comment. The conversation goes on as before. Later, when he is undressing for bed, Mother says: "By the way, Arthur, don't you remember that there is a custom that we don't talk about our physiological workings while we are at the table? We don't talk about the details of digestion or circulation or—"

"Or bloody noses," contributes Arthur.

Mother agrees. "Or the mechanics of the baby. Some things we keep among the family affairs to be discussed when the family is alone."

"It's a sissy idea," scorns Arthur. "I can eat just as well if people talk about blood and wrecks with a hundred people killed. But I'll remember."

Some weeks later when his mother is taken to the hospital Arthur's concern is very real. So is his intelligent comprehension— to the limits, of course, of a well-informed, interested nine-year-old. He asks whether the baby came head-first, whether its head was "squashed" badly, whether his mother suffered much. But after he has seen the baby (who proves to be a little sister, not much use as a future member of the ball team), after she has been brought home and he has assisted at her bath and commented on how complete she is while yet so tiny, he seems to have no further interest in the general subjct of sex and birth for several years.

An older child than Arthur, who already knows in a general way the role of father and mother in procreation and the basic facts of the process of birth, may become explicit in his interest in hereditary factors and in the various stages of embryological development. Then the parent may want to make fuller response.

"How did you begin to be you? That's a big question and the best answers we know are only partial, not to mention the limitation of our laymen's understanding. One thing we do know is that you began from your chromosomes, those tiny bodies of protoplasmic material within the nucleus of the first cell which was you. Your chromosomes were a direct gift from your parents carried in the sperm of the father and the egg of the mother. It's a world's wonder, really, that you are you because only one of the hundred million sperms carried in a single drop of seminal fluid could be used by any specific egg. If any other of the hundred million had met up with the particular egg which carried your maternal inheritance, then you would be different. You would be not-you.

"To pin down your beginning: when a sperm enters an egg it contains twenty-four of those closely packed chromosomes which are all the hereditary material contributed by the father and half of the material of you. The egg nucleus also contains its twenty-four chromosomes. When the two sets of twenty-four chromosomes unite, the resulting twenty-four pairs are your heritage for all time. Hereafter every cell in your body will contain forty-eight chromosomes, exact duplicates of those which made up your first cell. Mathematically, you might have expected forty-eight chromosomes from each parent since every cell of the human species contains that number. But the germ cells alone are able to effect a reduction division so that sperm and egg each contribute only one half the parents' quota of chromosomes. These two sets of chromosomes, forty-eight in all, might have united in a great number of combinations as you can figure for yourself whenever you have a couple of free years. One pair of parents could produce something like 16,777,216 different combinations of hereditary factors. By what narrow margin was Shapespeare achieved, or Caesar, or Plato, or Mozart, or you.

"This new cell which is you starts life in the mother's Fallopian tube, and there commences the most precarious few weeks of your existence. No matter whether you may later be shipwrecked, dropped from a parachute, detailed to the ocean floor or to the stratosphere, you will never again live nine days so hazardous as the time it took you, a pin-point egg, to make your perilous journey down the Fallopian tube to the vast, dark, brooding universe of the uterus. You arrived in the nick of time. But many of your brothers and sisters were no doubt lost before they were able to implant themselves along the lining of the uterus and set up a placental feed line. You were distinctly the exception in achieving a foothold in your new environment. Triumphant you!

"Do not think, though, that once you moved into your cozy habitat, your mother took over a direct feeding job and you ceased to work for your living. Actually you were on your own from scratch, always separate from your mother. Oliver Wendell Holmes once rendered a court decision to the effect that an unborn child was part of its mother but that decision was his mistake. From the moment your particular forty-eight chromosomes started out, you were a completely separate being at the mercy of your environment. None of your mother's blood ever reached you. The most she could do was to feed the placenta which lined the uterus. From its walls your food made its way to you by osmotic process; the same process by which a blotter soaks up ink.

"Whether you are male or female appears purely a

matter of chance, although your sex was determined in your first cell when egg and sperm united. The only difference between the chromosomes of a man and woman lies in a single chromosome of one pair. What might be called their A-pair are alike; their B-pair alike; their C-pair, D-pair, and so on. But one pair, which might arbitrarily be called the K-pair, are not alike. In the K-pair of a woman's chromosomes, each chromosome carries a factor we may call X. Thus it makes no difference which one of a woman's K-pair is contributed to the egg cell. In the corresponding K-pair of a man's chromosomes, one carries an X identical with the woman's X, but the other carries a factor we may call Y. If an X-sperm first get to the X-egg, then the resulting individual is an XX and eventually a baby girl will be born. If a Y-sperm unites with the X-egg, then the ultimate individual is a boy baby.

"There is more to this X vs. Y race. For some reason, the Y-sperms are more successful than the X-sperms; more of them reach the egg. Probably 20 per cent more males are formed than females and yet there are more female births. Embryologists figure that in approximately one-fourth of all known pregnancies the fetus is lost at some time during its development. From studies of thousands of embryos it appears that the loss is four times as great, for instance, among three-month male embryos as among female embryos. At four months the loss is twice as great. So on, at varying ratios, the male always has a harder time to survive. The drama of the sexes is epic.

"Actually the prologue of your life is made up of a play within a play because there is a highly exciting drama within the chromosomes of your first cell. How small can you think? Small as they are, chromosomes are elastic little somebodies; they stretch out into filaments that consist of gelatinous beads strung closely together. These beads either are or contain the ultimate factors of heredity called genes. There may be scores or even hundreds of genes in one chromosome which, you recall, originally filled one twenty-fourth part of the head of a sperm which was itself microscopic. And yet one gene may change the whole pattern of your life. Precarious you.

"Each gene has a job to do because genes are the builders of all that can ever be you. They determine your stature, the color of your eyes, the amount of your hair, the shape of your nose, the length of your toes. They give you your musical ability, your fondness for sports, your flair for mathematics, your lack of a sense of direction. The potentialities for every facet of you were set by your genes. Whatever your mother may have experienced while you dwelt within her body, she could not affect your gene pattern, although her poor health could decrease the food available for your growth. Also some diseases such as diphtheria, typhoid, syphilis, and influenza may penetrate the placenta and reach the baby's body so that it is infected before birth. But the baby cannot inherit the disease; it can only pick up the disease from its immediate prebirth environment. To be sure, your genes may build in you the same pattern of weak lungs which made it possible for one of your parents to pick up tuberculosis and which make you susceptible. Or you could be the victim of 'black' genes, meaning genes which carry destructive factors. But these 'black' genes can only come your way if they are a part of the chromosome pattern of your parents. And even then, many strains require double inheritance from both father and mother before the defect is built into a new individual. The laws for inheritance through genes are just as predictable and demonstrable as the laws which govern the movement of heavenly bodies or the behavior of chemical elements.

"Back there when you were a nine-day-old egg newly arrived in the vastness of the uterus—remember?—that was the time when you began to be a specialist yourself. Cells began to multiply and to differentiate until groups of cells having similar structure and performing specialized functions became various kinds of tissues. These tissues assembled themselves into organs or functional units. Organs grouped themselves into systems. For instance, the circulatory system is made up of heart and blood vessels with blood and lymph supply. It had to begin work on its own, but at the same time it also had to work in co-ordination with other systems—digestive, nervous, and the like. The specialists specialized in working together.

"At four months the embryo weighs around five ounces and measures six inches; brain convolutions are forming, sex is recognizable, muscles produce movement of the limbs. At five months, the embryo measures some ten inches and has doubled its weight of the previous month; hair and nails are forming. At six months weight has increased to a pound, eyelids with their eyelashes are formed but closed; fat gathers under the skin. At seven months the gain in weight is 300 per cent or more, and the three-to-four-pound fetus measures thirteen to fifteen inches; eyelids open. At eight months the length may be eighteen inches, the weight four to five pounds; nails are complete. All of this time blood supply is maintained between the placenta and the liver of the fetus by way of the umbilical cord. Lungs which previous to respiration are dense and solid nevertheless are thought by some to have convulsive movements, and a mouth which has as yet no use in food-taking may have a sucking movement. The day of birth is approaching.

"At the end of two-hundred-eighty days, or ten lunar months, the second tremendous event of your lifetime takes place: you are born. At one instant you were nobody, so far as the world of men, events, and statistics is concerned. The next instant you were somebody with rights, privileges, and responsibilities. A physiological process had produced a rational problem which has to work out its own meaning. You—weighted and freighted with destiny."

With certain children, the fuller the answer to a pressing question, the more ensuing questions are brought to the fore. But that is the blessed way with curiosity, one of life's most valuable gifts to the eager-minded. So, although a parent may let himself in for a lot of answer-hunting, he is giving his child a better gift than any conceivable *thing* when he offers answers which raise further questions. Some of these young questioners will set up new hypotheses by which the race may be able to advance in wisdom and stature, "in favor with God and man."

XI. What about the Teens?

*And yet there was the impressiveness of size about
him, especially about his legs and chin. At seventeen
and eighteen growth is still going on, sometimes in
a sporadic way, several parts seeming to have sprouted
faster than others. Often the features have not quite
settled down together in harmony, a mouth, for instance, appearing to have gained such a lead over the
rest of a face, that even a mother may fear it can
never be overtaken. Voices, too, often seem mis-
placed; one hears, outside the door, the bass rumble
of a sinister giant, and a mild boy, thin as a cricket,
walks in.*

BOOTH TARKINGTON (*Seventeen*)

It is in his second year in junior high that Arthur begins
to go with the boys from across Davis street. The new
boys come to the house freely. Sometimes they stay for
lunch and Arthur's mother makes them feel at home.
Arthur tries not to let on to her that he notices how they
"guzzle their soup" and sprawl over the table. They are
older than Arthur, all four of them, and obviously he
covets their approval. Both father and mother decide that
in this case it is better to supervise the friendship as best
they can and let it wear itself out.

One day Arthur appears in the library where his father
and mother are looking at a new book. He is embarrassed.
His face is flushed; he twists his cap in his hands.

"What is it, Arthur?" asks his father easily, sensing the
boy's apprehension.

"Oh, nothing," says Arthur. "I thought you were alone and I was just going to ask you something. But it isn't important." He turns away.

"I'm leaving anyway," says his mother quickly. "We're cleaning the pantry." As she goes through the door, she tousles his hair just the way she sometimes does to father's.

As soon as he is alone with his father, Arthur speaks in one gulp. "Those kids—Lem and Pinky and Toots and them—they say it's the bunk about one man and one woman and the baby business. They say somebody's fed me a lot of baby talk. They say every man has a lot of women and that he doesn't have them because the girls want babies either. They say there never was a man that didn't have his women a long time before he got married, too. Lem, he's tried it and Pinky's aiming to soon. They say you don't know a thing about fun until you find out what a girl's really for. They say there's a special way you do with girls so they won't get babies but they won't tell me what it is because you got to pay to get it."

Arthur stops, pale and shaken, emptied of these things he has been unable to digest.

"Sit down," says his father seriously. The boy sits, and for a moment neither speaks. Then his father's words come deliberately, sternly. But Arthur does not feel that the sternness is for him. Rather for the facts of which he speaks.

"Some of the things the boys have said are true. But those things have the same relationship to normal sexual relations that anarchy has to government." Father pauses for a moment. "It is true that sexual relations have other importance besides the desire for procreation, and having a family isn't the only reason that a man and a woman live together although most men and women do want to have children. There is the whole range of comradeship, the sharing of interests, hopes, plans, daily pursuits. Both are likely to be busy people and they treasure their time together. Sleeping together is a particularly comforting kind of nearness. Being able to reach out and touch someone you love is often more important than any words you can say to them, or they to you. And probably the highest point of this wordless understanding which flows between two human individuals is reached in the sex relation. It is the culmination of this feeling of oneness, a moment of complete fulfillment—to be treasured for its own sake, for the security and elation and peace it brings to the spirit, as well as for the fact that it may provide the physical basis of new life.

"Of course, there are cheap counterparts for most of life's rare gifts, this among the others. You realize, for instance, that a surgeon has it in his power to know a tremendous sort of exhilaration when he invents and performs a difficult operation—or he can find a degree of cheap exhilaration in a bottle of whiskey. He rates the value of each kind of exhilaration by the results, by the way he feels about the experience afterwards, by what it does for him. In something of the same fashion, there is a cheap counterpart for the full experience of the sexual relationship. It is true that a man may perform the same act with any other woman, no matter what her color or class or quality, and it will provide a physical thrill. The woman may be a stranger for whom he cares nothing at all. No affection enters into the deal; it may make no slightest difference to her who he is or what his real need may be. That's one kind of sexual experience. It seems to me that you pretty much have to choose in life which you will have—one woman of many. You can't have both. If, as these boys said to you, a man wants to go from woman to woman hunting a momentary thrill, he can get it. But if he does that, then he will never know the fullness of the peculiar bond which exists between a man and woman who belong exclusively to each other."

All the while his father is speaking, Arthur sits very still, intently watching his father's face. He seems to be taking in more than the words. He feels, without having words for the feeling, that there is a quality about his father which demands the best things from life. He feels there is an integrity in his father which puts the best back into life, a *noblesse oblige* of the human spirit to give and to take only the best. He wants to be like his father. When Arthur stands up to leave he feels taller. He also feels as if he has had a violent sickness and suddenly got well but is still weak—weak and strong, stronger than he ever felt before. All he says is, "Well, I guess I see now how it is," and then he goes upstairs to get ready for school.

Not all deleterious sex experience involves both sexes. A considerable number of children learn to masturbate, and this is one of the experiences about which questions are seldom asked, so that when help is needed parents have to devise a way to answer unexpressed needs. The causes of masturbation cover a wide latitude, ranging from mere curiosity aroused by some accidental stimulation of the sex organ to deliberate teaching by an older child. Probably most small children at some time become involved with other children who are secretively curious and experimental about their sex organs. A mother may notice her small son coming in from play flushed and irritable, not at all his direct self. A few questions usually bring out the difficulty. Ordinarily a sufficient method of dealing with the matter is for the mother to make a firm but unemotional statement that handling the sex organs is not a healthy habit. The child probably classes her disapproval with the dark frown she bestows on picking the nose or probing the navel. At the same time the mother needs to make sure that unsatisfied curiosity is not nagging the child, and she does well to keep an open eye toward making sure that the child plays where she can keep some tab on him. The experience may never be repeated. Or it may be repeated in a new context at some later time. If the problem becomes marked then the parents may need the help of a more experienced parent or of a doctor.

With teen-agers the best answer to the unspoken query as to why they should not masturbate is usually a full discussion of the physiology of sex. The more thoroughly an adolescent understands how his body functions, including his reproductive system with all its possibilities for misdirection, the more likely he is to further his own best interests. He knows it is *himself* on a physiological level with which he is dealing, and unless he has been pampered or otherwise taught disrespect to himself as a person, he tends to co-operate with nature's helpful laws as he understands them.

Many adolescent problems are rooted in childhood and only appear to shoot up suddenly in the tumultuous teens. Our parental hindsight is so much sharper than our day-to-day appraisal that we often feel we are walking backward through the maze of our days. Still—forewarned is forearmed, as our grandparents told us, and a parent who expects to be successful with teen-agers has to have a sharp eye, ear, and maybe tongue with the nine-to-eleven age. Take the matter of sex experience known as off-color or even abnormal which often comes to a child's attention through the sheer matter of vocabulary. Words are current, and used casually, which once would never have been heard among younger children of "good" families. Frequently the child does not even know what the words mean; he merely uses them. Sometimes a parent has to make the child conscious of the meaning of his vocabulary.

For instance, Bill, aged ten, coming home from school with a bloody nose and the spirited huff of one who has been unjustly dealt with. "Jack got mad when I called him a son-of-a-bitch. What's that to get so mad about? A bitch is a mother dog and a son of a bitch is a male puppy. Anybody ought to be glad to be a good pup. I could have called him a lot worse."

So we answer calmly, "But it's a word people never have liked to be called. Polite people never say it. You'd do well to drop it out of your vocabulary."

That's firm; that's unemotional; that's neat in us. But, it doesn't meet Bill's problem. He was asking why a person objects to being called a son-of-a-bitch. It is a phrase which he cannot escape; coin of the realm; meaning nothing much to half the boys who use it, but intended as a term of sharp degradation by the rest. Having asked, he has a right to know its meaning.

Son-of-a-bitch, obviously, is a sex-rooted phrase. And the only sure way to deal with words or experience related to abnormal sexual behavior is first to make sure that the child has a clear understanding of normal sex behavior. If the abnormal experience comes ahead of the normal instruction, then we have so much more difficult a task because we still have to make plain the normal before we can deal with the abnormal. The best insurance for handling any abnormality is a good old common-sense approach to the normal.

Bill is right, of course, in insisting that the term "bitch" means a female canine and that as such the word is in good repute. But the original Anglo-Saxon *bicce* also means a wanton woman, a meaning probably derived from the periodic promiscuity of dogs. And what is a wanton woman, a prostitute, a harlot, in terms a ten-year-old can understand? It is a woman who offers the physical act of belonging to a man without the mutual love which gives the act meaning. In terms adapted to the child's general knowledge and to his previous understanding of mating, a parent may need to review the meaning of marriage, and to make plain that a woman who goes around having intercourse with any man she chooses cheats three people: herself, the man to whom she gives the meaningless gestures of love, and the baby who may come and will probably never have a father's care.

Such a woman also cheats society. The word "society" may not be in a ten-year-old vocabulary, but the fact of society's interest in individual conduct and well-being is one with which a ten-year-old deals constantly. He knows that society is concerned with clean drinking water, safe driving, good street lights, plenty of teachers for the public schools. He can see that since society is concerned with the welfare of all children, then the welfare of the unwanted children of prostitutes, or bitches, matters particularly because these children have a more difficult time growing up to be good citizens than do the children of happily married parents. Also that the burden of their support and care is forced onto all of the people who must pay taxes to provide orphanages, clinics, and other public care.

All in all it becomes a grave matter to call any individual a son-of-a-bitch or a bastard. Even when the words are used lightly, still they are terms of dishonor, terms we resent when applied to ourself and consequently refrain from using. Some parents may feel, of course, that so long and grave a response is not called forth by the use of off-color sex phrases, but any logical opening for a parent to help keep sex experience in focus as an impersonal consideration helps by indirection at the personal level. A teen-ager, taking in the same facts regarding prostitution, can also be shown something of the problem of venereal disease, and of the problem, constantly brought to attention in news reports, of the sex maniac.

Probably no sex problem is harder for a child or an adolescent to bring into the open than that of sex deviation. However, at least by adolescence, a child is bound to run into the term "homosexual" and to hear many of the popular substitute words. Often he uses them without knowing their meaning. Sometimes we wonder whether it is better to open the subject by the time a child reaches adolscence or to wait until some incident brings the matter into the foreground of attention.

Some parents prefer to make sure that the young understand the problem by taking advantage of a natural opening in a conversation, or by making an opening to warn the child.

"You should know something about homosexuality because it leads to a great deal of grief and frustration in our society. You see, not everyone confines his or her sex interest to members of the opposite sex. For any of a number of mixed-up psychological reasons, some girls distrust the slightest expression of love interest from boys. A girl may feel that she should have been a man; she wants to protect and care for a more feminine girl. Or a very feminine girl may want sex attention but wants it 'safely' in a form which could not eventuate in children and family responsibility. And some boys feel repulsion toward girls, but still they have a sex drive, and so they try to satisfy their sex craving with members of their own sex. Sometimes a boy gets another boy to act as much like a girl as possible while he takes on the masculine protective role toward this male substitute for a sweetheart.

Or another boy may feel himself to be essentially feminine; he likes to wear fine fabrics and feminine colors; he wants to be looked after, petted, pampered, by a strong man.

"These unnatural 'couples' try to effect sex expression through various adaptations of the sex act. This kind of sex behavior leads to unhappiness and further maladjustment for many reasons. The participants feel guilty because they know they are under society's disapproval; their acts are illegal and hence if discovered may lead to a court sentence; also to loss of position and great difficulty in finding another position. So if anyone of your own sex, old or young, begins to cling to you, or to possess your time exclusively, or to show signs of physical intimacy, leave that individual alone. But if possible ask some competent adult to give the person counsel.

"And if you ever feel yourself peculiarly absorbed in curiosity regarding individuals of your own sex, don't think you are queer and try to keep your problem to yourself. You go right to someone whose counsel you value. For often some perplexity beneath the surface, something which has nothing to do with your customary conduct or interest, has driven you in this direction. Your real problem may be relatively easy for someone skilled in such understanding to handle. Adolescent emotions are easily mixed up, but with wise counseling they are often as easily straightened out. The important thing is not to blame anyone, but to get help."

Not all parents can bring themselves to broach the subject of homosexuality. They prefer to keep an appraising eye on their children's associates and to postpone discussion, hoping that the child may grow into adolescence without any particular curiosity on the subject and certainly without disastrous experience. And so the child may. By the later teens, such parents may feel, a young person is almost bound to come upon an adequate discussion of homosexuality in some magazine or book, in classroom discussion, or in talk with his better-informed contemporaries or with some dependable counselor. Or the parents may ask the school authorities to cover the subject in scheduled lectures on the general subject of sex.

In spite of counsel some boys and girls are caught off guard or are otherwise unable to protect themselves from unwanted sex experience. When a terrifying experience does occur, the first consideration is to get the whole story from the child. Help him to tell every detail, so that nothing remains hidden to fester in the depths of his mind, later to pour pus into his mental bloodstream. It may be very difficult for the child to tell the whole story, especially if some act of his own has precipitated a reaction he never dreamed of. His own guilt or his parents' embarrassment or recrimination may easily block the full recital. But a far-sighted parent will get the story out. A hidden terror is ten times the horror than an open terror, sanely dealt with, can ever be.

Then, once out, the parent can help the child to feel that his experience, however upsetting, is already in the past. Moreover, it has happened to others and their entire lives were not ruined. A bitter incident need not spoil, nor even appreciably scar, a child's life. Once an experience is delineated, accepted, and the child given the emotional security of his parents' understanding, then it can be related to his enlarging comprehension of human behavior. A large order for a child, but this is the kind of world, the kind of society, the modern child is born into. Success in dealing with abnormal sex behavior can be judged by the continuing openness of the channel of communication between parents and child. Remaining on a hearing level is a parent-child relationship compounded of love, imagination, and knowledgable common sense which will steady the child as he matures and finds his way among his own experiences with all the kinds of people who make up his life.

In helping the adolescent to find his way among the problems of sex, the parent surely cannot overlook the immediate physical manifestations of maturity with which the child has to deal. The sex urge may come so swiftly and disturbingly upon a boy or girl as to be overwhelming. Or it may upset his emotional balance without his knowing what is making him so irritable, so tired, so careless, so—any one of a dozen things.

Here again the parent can find much help for the child, and for himself, in books written with the particular purpose of explaining the physical and psychological changes of adolescence to the one having the experience. The parent need not be mysterious or heavy-handed about offering such books to the boy or girl. A mother, for instance, may meet an unwonted burst of irritability on the part of her daughter with the cheerful remark: "My stars, you must be sailing into the stormy waters of adolescence. Well, you may find some help for charting your course in a book that has helped me." (It is to be hoped that her words will sound less like a line learned from the book.) Or a father may say to his son: "You are growing so fast I can't keep track of you. Growing up has its special problems. I can't remember them all, and those I do remember may not be your problems. But there's a pretty good book on the whole business which will give you some pointers."

Each family has its own vocabulary, its own camaraderie, its own way of sharing confidences. But whatever the family characteristics, one thing the present-day parent can be sure of: his sons and daughters are likely to be flippant when they are in earnest, and very, very offhand about a thing in which they have deep concern. If the parent can come somewhere near to matching the child's mood, he stands a better chance of holding the child's confidence.

Both boys and girls need some explicit instruction on the matter of menstruation. Gone are the days when boys from "good families" frequently grew to maturity without any knowledge of this part of nature's preparation for parenthood. National advertising has taken care of part of the instruction, and the frankness with which many girls refuse a swimming date, for instance, with a casual, "Sorry, but not today," makes it impossible for a growing boy not to be aware of the problem.

It is probably more important that a mother anticipate the problem for her daughter. There have been, and still are, too many serious emotional consequences when a girl is suddenly overtaken by the menstrual flow and thinks she is the victim of some mysterious disorder or is dying of hemorrhage. Gone are the days—one hopes—when a mother takes her daughter into the darkened guest room and offers to talk to her "as one woman to another about a certain time of month when a lady doesn't do some things." Today, although some girls still suffer extreme discomfort during a menstrual period, most girls take it in their stride and are able to go right on with their daily routine of work and play. A mother can best treat the subject in that spirit.

It may be considerable help to call attention to the emotional rise and fall which accompanies the menstrual cycle. Just before menstruation many girls feel edgy and irritated, or depressed and discouraged; school work drags or overwhelms. But after menstruation energy appears to rise above average, creativity is high, responsibilities are easily handled. Knowing *when* to avoid arguments, stick to routine tasks, get extra sleep, and when to take on creative work, extra jobs, and personal adjustments, can be as important as knowing *how*. Menstruation is a major fact of a woman's life span, and giving her daughter sound physiological and psychological understanding may be one of a mother's best contributions to the next generation's equanimity.

When Effie is eleven her mother decides that it is time she know about menstruation. Not only is the child maturing but she is going about with older girls; she should be saved the embarrassment of being the uninformed one. Her mother wishes a logical moment would present itself. She hesitates to say, while Effie is practicing on the piano or washing her socks, "Oh, by the way, there is something you need to know." But as always the child makes her own opportunity. Effie in her snowsuit, dripping melted snow, drops down on a rug in front of the fire.

"Gretchen's getting to be an awful sissy. This is about the fourth time that we've started off skating or sliding or something and she's said, 'I can't chase around today.' She makes it sound mysterious. I hope I never get like that."

"You may, though," says Mother. "If she feels the way I do today, she has a perfectly good excuse for not chasing around, and if you'll take off your wet snowsuit before it makes puddles on the rug I'll tell you something interesting."

Effie dispenses with the wet suit and comes back munching an apple. "What's brewing?" she asks with interest.

"Gretchen's probably beginning to experience nature's preparedness program," says Mother. "Nature begins quite early to get a woman ready for the business of having a family. You remember that when a woman is carrying a baby, she has to furnish the food for the growing fetus, indirectly, from her own blood stream. It takes a good deal of food, too, which is another way of saying it takes a good deal of blood and strength. If the mother's body had that drain put on it all at once, she would lose more energy than she could afford to part with. So nature has a way of beginning, when a girl is about twelve or thirteen, to store up extra blood each month. The blood collects in the uterus which, you remember, is the organ the baby lives in during the nine months of pregnancy. But when there is no baby, the uterus has no need of this extra food supply of blood. So it empties itself about once in twenty-eight days."

"Good night!" says Effie in alarm. "I hope it gives some warning. What if you were at school or out playing and a lot of blood rushed out?"

"It doesn't happen all at once. For about three days, sometimes longer, a little blood keeps seeping. Usually a girl knows by watching the calendar which day it will begin and she protects her clothes by wearing a sanitary pad. You see them advertised in many magazines."

"I wondered what those were," says Effie. "I was going to ask you."

"I'll show you when we go upstairs. In fact, I'll give you some so that you'll have them handy if you should begin to menstruate when I'm not around."

"Does it hurt? I mean do you feel like you'd had an awful cut or something?"

"Gracious, no. Nature is a better engineer than that. The whole process is as mechanical as digestion and when a girl lives a healthy normal life, she is not much more conscious of it than of her digestion."

Effie looks contemplative. Then her eyes light up and she remarks, "I think it's a slick idea that nature figured out. Gretchen needn't have been so mysterious about it."

"It's nothing to shout about either. Just what you call 'one of those things.' First time I think of it I'll look up a good book for you, one that describes the whole complicated mechanism of menstruation. In fact, I'd like to read one again myself."

The conversation terminates with Effie's feeling a little more grown up and a little better acquainted with her mother. Being forearmed with knowledge, she has the security of which she does not even need to be conscious.

The physiological problems of growing up are not the only problems the adolescent faces. There are also new problems of social adjustment. The boy not only is awkward; he knows he is awkward. Also he hears his voice performing strange antics. The girl frequently realizes that she is neither a child nor a woman. As surely as she acts grown up, someone calls attention to the fact that she is only a child.

A thoughtful parent can save his child some of these embarrassments. He can anticipate the child's needs and help to ease him into the grow-up status. It is difficult, for instance, for a boy to ask for his first razor. If there are younger brothers and sisters, they are likely to shout, "Ernie's learning to shave!" As if Ernie doesn't feel conspicuous enough. Fortunately, in the actual case of Ernie, his mother sensed his embarrassment over the heavy down appearing on his face and spared him annoyance from his younger brothers by saying, in their hearing, "Ernie, I do wish you'd shave and not go around looking like a stubble field." She put some asperity into her voice. "You always used to take more trouble with your looks."

The next day she brought home the shaving equipment

and said, again in the presence of the younger children: "You can't put off shaving indefinitely. It's just one of the things men have to do, and if you need to begin younger than some, that's merely your hard luck." Still grumbling a bit, she left Ernie to examine this implement for which he had been waiting. And when he went off to use it, there were no comments from the rest of the family.

Girls swing more readily into their beautification programs. Any time from twelve on, they party-out for a dance, and the next thing a parent knows lipstick and nail polish are daily routine. No girl ever took easily to high heels, no matter how deep the longing to stilt across a room. Any parent who has looked in on first-day receptions at prep schools realizes how uncertain a girl can feel in hose, heels, and the necessity to cross a room.

Whether the accoutrements of adulthood are heralded with, "Must I, Mother?" or "Why can't I, Mother?" there is still the bridge from childhood to young-ladyhood to cross. A poet of an older day named it, "Standing with reluctant feet where the brook and river meet."

"Must you meet my date, Dad?" Whether the question is stated or hidden behind anxious eyes, many a girl is overwhelmed at the realization that her father will be sizing up her escort. First escorts are likely to seem so young, even to a girl of the same age, that the girl feels as if she'd been caught cradle-snatching. Blessed be the offhand fathers who do not overjoke, overentertain, talk down, show solicitude, caution the "children" when to be in, completely ignore them, proffer advice, comment on how lovely the daughter looks, pass a withering word, act as if the boy were a rival, a thief, a dunce, or an accident of nature. What *can* a father do in answer to his daughter's unspoken appeal for assurance? He can take a long,

long look at the Golden Rule. A fine exercise for the imagination, a father trying to sense how that inexperienced daughter feels.

A boy needs just as much reassurance. To decide to spend his allowance or his hard-come-by cash on a girl is decision enough, but then there is the matter of what kind of corsage, whether to send or take it, whether to pin it on the girl or thrust it into her hands, what to say to her parents, how to treat the younger fry or, even worse, the older brothers and sisters, how to get her safely out the door, whether to allow his father to drive them to the party if he cannot take the car out alone, or to get a taxi, or walk. What to talk about! Whether to touch her, how to avoid it, how much to dare.

Often it comes as a shock to a father to see his son, especially a first son, taking off for a first date. A date— him? That means childhood has passed, and the father may never have had time to be a good father; not in the way he had meant to be. Well, this is his second chance. At adolescence when a boy begins to take the making of himself into his own hands, a father also has a fresh opportunity to take the making of their relationship into his own hands.

With adolescence, a parent may be a successful answerer and never know what made him successful; he can also be a colossal failure and never know exactly what made him fail. But failure is a lot less likely with parents who take time to think about life the way it looks to the child, including the parent relationship the way it must look to the child.

XII. What about Marriage?

Ice cream is a very strange thing,
And so is a codfish ball,
But the people people marry
Is the strangest thing of all.

Quite apart from considerations of sex, children have a good many questions to ask about the institution of marriage. They build up their attitude toward marriage by incidental and personal interrogation. "Why did you marry Daddy? What did he say when he asked you?" "But, Dad, how could you have been practically engaged to her? Either you were or you weren't." "If Daddy doesn't cut the grass, why don't you get another Daddy for a while? And then he'll be sorry." "Why do Mr. and Mrs. Rumpus keep living in the same house when they argue all the time?" "Why does a family all have to live in the same house? Couldn't there be a children's house and a grown-up's house?" The gamut of questions is wide and curious, and the answers might not be particularly important were it not that the child has a way of piecing together the garnered information into something of a pattern for living.

With the mid-teens and the upwelling of the sex drive, which is a terrific new experience in itself, comes also the sudden impingement of social conventions which previously have seemed inventions by adults for adults. What the adolescent does is all at once the business of a lot of people, some of whom he cares about but many of whom are as immaterial in his consideration as so many trees. And yet these people make up "society" which apparently has authority to curtail his expression of himself.

One pressing question always relates to the degree of familiarity advisable between boys and girls. Where does one draw the line between the normal, hearty give-and-take of boys and girls who share their tennis, swimming, picnics, dancing, school life and other interests, and the personal familiarities between one boy and one girl?

One parent says to a daughter, "Familiarity is pretty much a matter of taste. Personalities which set high value on their own worth are not likely to permit actions which seem common. A fair standard is: do not do the thing which makes you feel shopworn afterward. And by all means trust your first negative reactions; an experience which goes against the grain is not for you."

Another parent says to a son: "When it comes to petting, look at the situation as if you were someone else— someone you admire very much—in your place. If the action doesn't seem in keeping with this person whom you admire, then it is probably not for you."

A third parent, attempting to take a long view, may generalize. "If your actions became the social standard, do you feel society would be distinctly benefited? Considering the fact that there are so many kinds of human nature, would you say that your standards are 'best for the most in the long run'?"

A thoroughly realistic parent may wish to be explicit. "Of course there's nothing the matter with kissing *per se*. As you say, these days everybody kisses everybody. Among adults the gesture may mean no more than an acknowledgment that the two are pleasant acquaintances, or merely that they wish to pass as such. It is not the fact of a kiss that you need to question but the meaning and what it leads to. Kissing your sister is probably a mark of affection, and it certainly has no overtones of passion. If a boy kisses his favorite girl friend in broad daylight in front of her house with her parents sitting on the front porch, he is probably absent-minded, showing off, or daring them to interfere. However, if he kisses her on that same porch in the moonlight, no parents present, and the kissing goes on for hours, he is rousing his own passions and hers. He is making love. He has embarked on the first steps of sexual expression which lead ultimately to the sex act, the act of physical union. The path is just that direct. It is an old path, well marked by the experience of millions. Moreover, it is a good path. The question for you is, when do you want to travel it? If you keep goading yourself, a little further with each experience, there comes a time when it is almost impossible to apply the brakes. Now maybe you say you will never get that far, but I tell you there is your nervous system to reckon with. Interest in sex becomes excessive when unsatisfied. If it cannot travel the normal path of satisfaction, then it may drive one down deviate paths.

"Look among your friends at the habitual and persistent heavy-daters, by whatever current name you call them. They are seldom top students, no matter how good their past record. They are seldom good mixers or real leaders over a long period. The reason may not be any lack of personal endowment, but energy is all one and it cannot flow in the other channels when it is being drained off in sexual interest. You might as well be realistic because this is the way human beings are geared. When boy-girl friendships remain generalized, the love-making light and limited, then the young personality has a chance to develop in an all-round fashion. But heavy petting of a premature sort penalizese the petters. So I tip you off—keep your interest wide, your sights high, your friendships deep, but until you are ready to consider marriage, keep most of your kisses on ice, and believe me, you'll find you're banking happiness."

Of course when boys and girls get into college or have full-time jobs they are likely to feel they are ready for love. For some a day then comes when they need an answer to the question as to what their attitude shall be toward sexual relations before marriage. The time has passed when all girls of "good families" accepted virginity as a qualification for marriage. On the other hand, the time has also passed when boys of good families had affairs before marriage but expected the girls whom they married to have a stainless past.

There are a number of studies on the sex attitudes and habits of college boys and girls and of young people in various occupational groups. They make plain three things: that there is no single accepted code of sexual conduct; that the proportion of young people having sexual experience before marriage runs higher than most parents surmise; that a considerable number of young people put other qualifications ahead of virginity as most desirable in a marriage partner.

The parent who wants to give his child a useful answer to this question of sex relations before marriage has to bear in mind these statistical findings and to realize that they speak for the generation of which his child is a part. Obviously, the standards have changed and it is to be expected that practically the entire age-group of fifteen to twenty-five are in some way affected by the change. The fact that young people ask the question what their attitude shall be toward sexual experience before marriage is proof that they are not sure of the answer; they are weighing the evidence.

Actually, of course, few young people approach their parents for advice on their sex life. They may talk freely with some other adult, if the occasion is exactly right. But more than likely the parent has to get his point of view into a general discussion—if he is fortunate enough to get in on the bull sessions of the young on occasion—or to move by indirection, seeing to it that the high school has a conference on marriage and the home or that adequate talks are given to the students. Some high schools and a considerable number of colleges have such conferences, addressed by experts and broken down into discussion groups in which the young talk freely indeed.

Some young people frankly advocate a casual attitude toward sex experience. Often, unknown to them—as a marriage adviser is likely to point out—their promiscuity is a manifestation of their need for prestige, or a desperate attempt to count with someone, an antidote for intense inner loneliness which may never become apparent in their extraverted behavior but is nevertheless a determining factor. Or it may be a reflection of gang mores, a very strong determinant in certain groups (not all of them among the underprivileged) in which a virgin, girl or boy, cannot "belong" to the inner circle.

Other young people uphold premarital experience only for a couple who honestly anticipate matrimony. They feel that an engagement "is the same as marriage" in intention, and that when a couple are held back from formal marriage by the necessities of their educational program, or by economic restrictions, or by some other consideration which they cannot presently override, there is no good reason why they should be denied this culminating expression of their love for each other.

An observant parent is likely to point out that there is no sharp line between these two groups—the advocates of a casual attitude toward general sex experience and the advocates of sexual freedom for the engaged couple—because many engagements of the very young go by the board; so then a second love affair ensues, a second breakdown, and so on, until an attitude of "what's the difference" develops, not only toward premarital experience but toward marriage. Without intent, an individual with such a history becomes a part of the promiscuous segment of the population.

A counseling parent may want to bring out the fact that there are always some in every generation who feel that the variety of their sex experience is a mark of broadmindedness, of sophistication; that among them are some intellectuals, some social experimenters and innovators, a much larger group with a low intelligence rating, the borderline cases designated as morons, the congenital malcontents unsure of what they want in life either for themselves or for society; that also among the promiscuous are a great many who have small consideration for the involvement of the partner, and of course smaller consideration for the baby who not infrequently complicates a temporary liaison. Before a young person commits himself to this pattern, or drifts into this way of life, he does well to look over the representatives of this group and conclude whether he honestly thinks his chance for long-run happiness is increased by becoming one with them.

The counselor may further want to point out that one great advantage of the wedding ceremony's coming ahead of the actual marriage is that the founding of the new home takes on dignity. Family, friends, well-wishers participate in an experience in which the imponderable elements of high expectation, hope for the future, pledge to each other, and request for the blessing and direction of God, probably outweigh the ponderable matters of house and livelihood. Then, too, a marriage ceremonially instituted impresses the participants as a wholehearted venture, entered into without a time-clause reservation. Hence disagreements, tensions, hardships are measured against the years and both parties have an impetus to work out harmonious adjustment. The odds are with the marriage which follows the pattern society has worked out as most compatible to the needs of most people.

Even so there are problems enough, for the young are seldom selfless, often fearful, frequently untested when it comes to making and spending money, balancing work, play and outgoing service, adjusting—but not too much— to the expectations of their comrades, parents, society in general. Every possible aid from society, including dignified privacy for sexual adjustment, should be gratefully accepted.

But other questions than sex are pertinent to a successful marriage and as adolescents approach the marriage age they begin to sense these considerations and to realize that they are not merely questions about the welfare of society in general but about their own immediate and personal welfare.

High school days are often the time when the question of interfaith marriage first rises. A Protestant boy dates a Roman Catholic girl, say; casual friendship ripens into "going steady," and then one day before Commencement they find themselves talking of marriage "some day." The girl, suddenly aware where she is headed, says, "But you'll have to become a Catholic." The boy laughs. "Shades of my grandfather! He was a Methodist minister. Our family have been Methodists ever since Wesley, I guess. Look, either you turn Methodist or else we'll each just stick to our own faith." But of course for the Catholic girl, that is an impossibility. Her only possible adjustment would be for the boy to take instruction in her faith and promise that all children who may bless the marriage will be reared as Catholics. Even so, she must work all of her days for his conversion.

If the boy acquiesces to the Catholic dominance, then he faces the grief of his family and a lifelong pattern of denying his own religious convictions. Moreover, any children they may have, compelled by their parents' vows to follow their mother's faith, will be inclined to feel that their father's religion is second class, not worth standing up for; or that he is outside the pale; or else to grow rebellious that they are not permitted to follow in his footsteps. And if they become defiant enough to refuse to go with the mother, then she has to live with an uneasy conscience and to accept a good deal of outside pressure. On the other hand, if the girl makes the adjustment and gives up her church, then she grieves her family, and may also feel adrift, deprived of a priest to make decisions for her on matters of faith and conduct. Whichever partner makes the adjustment, unless there is a true conversion, marriage is handicapped for unanimity at deep level of religious commitment is lacking; the parents have a differing philosophy of life which affects attitudes in multitudinous matters.

The same tension results from Roman Catholic - Jewish marriages, except that here each partner is committed to lifelong effort to convert the other. A Protestant - Jewish marriage also faces an initial handicap for the Jewish partner in that the rabbi is not permitted to perform the service and an orthodox Jewish family cannot recognize a service performed by a Protestant minister. If both partners remain true to their faith then there is also the divided loyalty of the children to reckon with.

According to studies made of mixed marriages, the tendency is for one or both parents to forego church attendance. One partner, at least, is likely to decide that the struggle, however amiably handled on the surface, is too much of a strain; better to let the other parent carry the religious responsibility. Which again leaves the children to decide who is "right," or which parent is weak.

No doubt the time to question interfaith marriage is before dating ripens into love. But this is a delicate matter, too. A Jewish parent hesitates to decree, "You simply cannot date non-Jewish boys; at least not in any steady fashion." A Protestant parent hesitates to say, "Look, son, Rebecca is a lovely girl but the religious beliefs and commitments of her family are entirely different from ours. Suppose you look elsewhere before you become too much involved." A Roman Catholic parent is less likely to hesitate to impose a hard and fast rule, but nevertheless many a Catholic parent grieves inwardly over having to cut short a budding romance between two young people who seem in every other way well suited.

In the end the best a parent can do is to point out the handicap under which an interfaith marriage operates. The ultimate decision rests with the couple themselves. And the patent fact that there are many distinguished interfaith marriages is proof that there can be no final ex-cathedra judgment. Fine personalities adjust sensitively, with mutual respect and a fair degree of open-minded consideration each for the other. All the argument in the world, and even the statistics which point plainly enough the liabilities of mixed marriage, do not obviate the successes.

In a different category are the interracial marriages. And here again young people are likely to fall in love before they ask their questions. A handsome young Indian comes as an exchange student; his classmates make him welcome; he attends college functions; the girls dance and date with him. After all he is as Aryan as they and probably as fine-featured; only his skin, eyes, and hair happen to be dark. Then he falls in love with a fair North American and she with him. He approaches her family—although probably he first approaches his own, for the dismay of the American parents, no matter how acute, is likely to be less than the consternation of his own. Although conceivably both families may eventually agree that the decision rests with the young couple themselves, there is still the matter of lifelong social pressure with which to reckon, as severe in one culture as in the other.

Nevertheless, notwithstanding social variances and personal difficulties, as more American students travel abroad, more young men in the armed forces go on foreign duty, more foreign students enter American institutions, more Negro-white equality is manifest in all aspects of national life, more interracial marriages are bound to take place. "Will we be sorry?" the young couple asks some trusted friend. "Will our children be penalized?" "How can standards be made more intelligent if intelligent people continue to abide by stupid conventions?" "Why should love pay the price exacted by ignorance?" "With our lifelong happiness at stake, what shall we do?"

In answer a few generalities apply. If both families agree to accept the partner of the other race, the first hurdle is passed. If both partners have a family background of education and general open-mindedness, the chances for happiness increase because the parents, as they become grandparents, are less likely to press for conformity to their own mores. If the young couple can set up their home in a cultural pattern which does not completely deprive either one of his traditional customs, food, language, companionship with fellow nationals, then the marriage has a better chance. For instance, an American girl married to a Korean man is less likely to feel a complete and devastated stranger in moments of marital or environmental stress if she lives in Seoul where life is somewhat westernized and American friends available than if the couple lives in a remote village where the Korean culture is relativly unyielding and she seldom hears English spoken except between her husband and herself. Likewise a Pakistinian man married to an American girl will probably find himself—and his marriage—happier if the couple lives near a university habitually attended by Pakistinians whom he can invite in for talk in his own language and food of their mutual preference; or perhaps near an oil installation where other Pakistinian engineers are constantly coming and going. A complacent, and perhaps bigoted, American town might prove wearing on Pakistinian broad-mindedness and hence wearing on the marriage.

A common religious affiliation is a great asset to an interracial marriage. Likewise common cultural interests— delight in music, facility in painting, enjoyment of the theater, the same literary taste. Regard for the same friends! Also shared hobbies—and it does not much matter whether they are mountain climbing, stamp collecting, photography, sailing, furniture repair, silverwork, gardening, or playing horshoes, except that a hobby which can be pursued while the wife is pregnant and while the husband is place-bound by his business has a continuing feasibility. A common attitude on social issues is of the essence, for racial tolerance ties in with many other social problems. But what the two have in common is no more important than what each has within himself. If each is a mature resourceful individual, happy when alone, equal to emergencies, capable of handling money intelligently, the chances of marital happiness are increased.

In a sense the Negro-white marriages are presently the most difficult, for there is none of the element of romance inherent in moving into a strange culture, and adjusting to obviously strange customs. There are only constant stupidities, injustices, discriminations on both sides of the racial barrier. Among educated young people, the best chance for happiness probably lies in living and working with such a group as the Friends. Which is not to say that other denominations than the Quakers do not cultivate racial tolerance, or that other professions than social service do not accept individuals for what they are and what they can do, but that a tradition of racial equality is a backlog against chilly experience.

Gone are the days when intelligent people put up arguments for the inherent anthropological superiority of this race or that, but the practice of treating people of all races with the respect accorded by the physical and social sciences is not yet widespread. Hence the best that a parent can do is to answer gravely regarding interracial marriage, that love and justice can wage a mighty battle for happiness, that courageous and honest parents are likely to have courageous and resourceful children who will manage their share of the pioneering, but that interracial marriage still faces enormous difficulties which require more selflessness than most young people possess.

At least one further question about marriage plagues the young where a generation or two ago it was seldom raised. "Why should we wait until we can support ourselves?" Two wars, but especially the Second World War, lowered the marriage age for thousands who formerly would have expected to wait until they were self-supporting. During the war young people felt justified in snatching their happiness when it offered and letting the future take care of its own problems. Moreover, as in no other generation, the girl could readily become a wage earner. And the boy, upon return, could look forward to governmental aid in continuing his education, or buying a farm, or getting into a small business of his own. And the parents, wrung by the dangers their sons and daughters faced, often acquiesced and helped to underwrite the new family.

Thus a pattern was set, and the next generation of students asked themselves and their elders why the cut of the cloth did not fit their needs as well. After all, a college generation is only four years; traditions are quickly set up. So many young people are not now waiting to fulfill their long professional training, or to make a down payment on a home, or to see their way clear financially before taking on the responsibilities of marriage. Still they are likely to talk things over with their elders.

In reply one parent may caution a son, "You're on your own when you marry. A man who takes on responsibility for a family has to be a mature citizen, financially independent." And he can document his point by showing the relationship between the ability to earn and spend money soundly and the ability to make the major decisions of family life; between the ability to share household tasks and the ability to ensure family humor, sanity, and justice.

But another parent may decide that since the girl his son has chosen has the making of a fine woman he is willing to share responsibility, at least financially, for the maturing process of both the young people. He may also feel that an early marriage has the most chance for continuing adaptability; perhaps also that once the young get the marriage question settled they can give their minds more wholeheartedly to their future professional training.

The big point about the time to marry, so far as the interfamily relationship is concerned, is to talk it out to the point of unanimity of decision if at all possible. When parents have no I-told-you-so upon which to fall back, and the young couple has no why-didn't-you-keep-me-from-it, then hardships are not so hard. For after all, marriage *is* a family affair, no matter how rugged the individualism, and the larger family unit is a great social shock absorber —when it remains a unit.

Fortunate the young people who have a place and opportunity to raise these questions before they become personal concerns and to work out meridian lines of conviction for use in future navigation. In this kind of answering before the question rises parents can often help most by indirection, possibly by making sure that the high school or college of which their sons and daughters are a part has adequate discussions, under expert direction, of the many considerations involved in marriage. Often churches and synagogues offer such counseling; frequently summer camps afford lectures and supervised bull sessions.

But no matter how carefully the young may think out such considerations in general, when they themselves are caught in the predicament of approaching marriage by a nonorthodox route, their problem is *new*. This is the time when parents say more with an attitude of objectivity and the old-fashioned emotions of tender concern and stanch faith in the young people themselves than in the wisest of words. To answer desperation without dogmatism, innovation without overestimating authority as such, apparent folly without distrust of the future merely because it is untried, requires a great deal of parental self-control. But that kind of control becomes farsightedness and keeps families together.

In regard to marriage, one of the most important areas

in a child's life, and certainly in an adolescent's life, is an area in which it is difficult for him to ask questions, namely, his parents' marriage. Although it is axiomatic that young people are conditioned to a happy or stressful marriage of their own by the quality of their parents' marriage, still they rarely realize that they are being permanently conditioned by the relationship of their parents to each other. The aphorism which states that a child is the center of the home certainly expresses the child's point of view; he sees his parents in relation to himself, not to each other.

Naturally children know that marriages break up, and they accept the fact in the abstract as part of the current scene, but when the marriage of their own parents breaks down, the experience usually comes as a definite shock. Even when they are prepared, in a sense, by observation of increasing discord, by threats, hints, and bitterness on the part of one or both parents, still the actual splitting asunder of family relationships shakes the foundations of their life. In a world already precarious and impermanent, why must this thing happen to *them*? Or if their world seems solid, permanent, satisfactory, then the shock is the greater. Caught in the predicament, children begin to question. Why, why, why? What about me? And parents have to answer.

A thorough explanation, geared to the child's years, may save a lasting trauma. Particularly with an adolescent all the ramifications of doubt, misunderstanding, distrust of either parent need to come into the open. After as much as possible is explained, parents may feel that they have to say, "Now we won't discuss this matter again." Certainly there is nothing to be gained by the customary procedure of a parent's self-justification manifest by rethrashing emotional scenes or by post-mortem agonizing. Explanations in words can be important; they can also confuse the issue. It is the continuing attitude of each parent toward the other and the ensuing conduct which count.

Dolly Mae Duggan lived with her parents and brother in a small yellow house; a trim sweet house with a trim sweet lawn. That is, from the outside all was trim. The outside was her father's responsibility, and Mr. Duggan was a trim, exact, dependable man. He worked in a garage and made excellent wages because he always did meticulous work. He liked everything around him neat, in place, orderly. Mrs. Duggan was not trim. She had not been trim when her husband married her but at that time he was fascinated by red-gold hair which curled of itself, by white hands, blue-blue eyes and a carefree laugh. Dolly Mae also liked her mother's laugh. But she did not like the way her mother kept house in spurts. When her mother had a clothes-washing spurt she washed everything on the place, including curtains and bathroom rugs. But she might not have another washing spurt for quite some time. She also cooked in spurts. Certainly she saw no sense in having dinner on the table exactly at six o'clock six days a week, which was the precise time her husband was ready to sit down at the table. Dolly Mae herself liked to eat at six o'clock; she found herself feeling empty as the clock moved toward six.

Mr. and Mrs. Duggan haggled a good deal. Dolly Mae was inclined to feel on her father's side when they haggled; but then she looked like her father, thin and trim and energetic. They haggled until Dolly Mae was eleven and Pete was eight. Then quiet Mr. Duggan decided he would rather be married to the cashier at the garage, a plain woman, but as trim as Mr. Duggan's hedge. The cashier did everything on time and was a good manager besides. She lived alone with her mother who was also neat and very precise, although rather an invalid.

When Mr. Duggan announced his transfer of loyalty and the filing of his bill of particulars against his wife, Mrs. Duggan wept for days; copious wet tears. She loved her husband. The haggling had never bothered her much; her mind wasn't really on it. What would people say? How could she ever support the children? Don't let the children worry her, Mr. Duggan said. She wouldn't have the children; he wouldn't have his children brought up by such a haphazard, make-shift et cetera. But of course the court gave her the children, along with a fair share of Mr. Duggan's wages, but not enough to live as comfortably as formerly. Mrs. Duggan wept on.

Dolly Mae had nothing to say. She couldn't comfort her mother exactly because everything her father said was true; only some way his accusations didn't seem as important as he made them sound. On the other hand, she couldn't side with her father, when the judge out-and-out asked her, because then it would seem as if her mother was dead. Every morning when she woke up she was sick at her stomach. She got very thin. She couldn't say she was mad at anyone, unless it was the children in her grade who kept asking her what had happened. Her mother saw that she was simply not herself; she scarcely ever wanted to go play. Pete, on the other hand, played all the time. He wouldn't do his household chores any more. He began to answer back to his mother. "Try and make me," he'd taunt her. Twice Mrs. Duggan threatened automatically that she would tell his father, but Pete slashed back, "I don't have a father any more."

"Yes you do," his mother corrected him.

"If he was my father he'd live with me." And Pete slammed out the door.

And then one day, about two months after the divorce, Mrs. Duggan did a surprising thing; "out of character," many would have said, except that beneath her lazy ways

Mrs. Duggan rather had character. While Dolly Mae and Pete were having their Saturday morning breakfast she sat down at the kitchen table beside them—last night's dishes being piled in the sink—and told the children that their father had had quite a point. She told them he was a good man, only very very very set in his ways. She'd always thought, vaguely, that she could change him and make him more easygoing to live with, but now she knew that kind couldn't change. Never mind; her kind could change when they had to. So—she had decided she was going to sell their father his own house, so to speak, the court having awarded it to her and the children; he and his wife could live in it. And then she and the children would live on the payments for the house, instead of on alimony, while she took a beauty culture course. She and the children would take a good convenient apartment. Moreover, she wanted the children to get over their rebellion about having to live with their father three months of the summer; she wanted them to drop in to see him evenings sometimes.

So Mrs. Duggan went to work. Dolly Mae did more of the housework but she didn't mind. She wasn't sick at her stomach any more. In time she and Pete began to pay short evening visits to their father and his neat trim wife and his neat rasping mother-in-law who did not wish to be called grandmother. For a while Dolly Mae kept a diary in which she only noted the advantages and disadvantages in her father's new set-up, until she outgrew the diary because her own life was too absorbing to pay much attention to his. For one thing, she helped look after Pete. He minded her, too. Pretty soon her mother said that she did declare, Pete did so many helpful things it was just like having a man around the apartment.

Everyone said that the first Mrs. Duggan, being a pretty

woman and the dependent type, would remarry before she finished her course. Dolly Mae heard the talk and it made her sick in her stomach again. But her mother only laughed at such nonsense. She said, "Once burned, always scarred," but not as if the scar were too painful. And up to the present age of forty-one Mrs. Duggan has not remarried. She really had loved her husband. Once when Dolly Mae was sixteen and had her first steady date, her mother told her that now she knew she had always taken her marriage for granted, as something nothing could change. Her own parents always haggled, she said, and they would never any more have thought of separation than of murder. She hoped Dolly Mae would marry a man she wouldn't need to haggle with. Mrs. Duggan made Dolly Mae and Pete a fine comfortable home, rather on the neat trim side, but always hospitable so that they could have their friends up any time and there was always room for one more. At twenty Dolly Mae married happily. Pete is in college. Mrs. Duggan is a very good beauty operator.

All in all that Duggan divorce scarcely maimed the children, due to the uncommon common sense and dignity and gumption of a woman whom many would have called haphazard and not very well educated. She answered a lot of questions her children never put into words—questions about responsibility, and making the best of hard circumstances, and not blaming someone else, and getting full joy out of each day, and co-operation and generous-mindedness. Maybe her greatest quality, though, was honesty.

Perhaps in a divorce situation no quality is more rare or more helpful than complete honesty.

Dora, off at prep school, sensed that all was not right at home. Although her parents made an extra effort to give her a good time during her weekends at home, she felt uneasy. A chum had whispered, a cousin had told her, and besides she just felt. So she asked her father.

She said, "I know you and Mother aren't very happy and I heard you are going to leave her and marry someone else. Is that true?"

Her father looked at her bewildered frightened eyes and had no tongue for the thing he had been trying to tell her for weeks. "Of course not," he said flatly. "We don't get along too well but her trip west doesn't mean a thing but a trip west."

Dora threw her arms around his neck and wept out all the anxieties of the past weeks. She went back to school.

Three days later she got a letter from him postmarked New York. "I was chicken; I couldn't tell you. The divorce came through yesterday. Tomorrow I'm being married and my new wife and I are flying to Europe. Please don't be upset. You're going to like her when we get back."

Dora spent two days in the school infirmary, first in hysterical grief and then under sleeping pills. "He lied; he lied," she kept saying. "I could have stood it if he hadn't lied."

In the ensuing months her mother's bitterness was no help in assembling a shattered young personality. Dora's marks dropped; she began to overdate and then to sneak out on promiscuous dates; she herself became a cheat and a liar. When the principal accused her she looked him in the eye and said, "Sure, I lie. My father lies, too." The words sounded strange coming from a sweet-faced girl, brought up in what would be called a sheltered home. Now Dora is seventeen. Her outlook for happiness is not bright. No one can add the final sum yet, but it looks as if someone should carve on the tombstone of her parents marriage: Honesty is not the only safeguard in presenting the hazardous facts of divorce to the young, but it is a tremendous advantage.

Of course, some of a child's most poignant questions about divorce are never asked. Johnny is twelve, bright as tacks, accustomed to boarding school and summer camps. His mother, at forty, has just married for the third time and is starting to Europe for the summer. Johnny comes home from school and says to the cook, "I wonder who I visit now till camp opens." He isn't really questioning; this kind of pillar-to-post life is his routine; he finds a degree of security within the pattern, such security as he gets. His mother says brightly, "Johnny likes to be on the go." How would she know? He has never had any opportunity to be other than on the go; he doesn't even question "the go."

What can parents say to questioning children except, in effect, "We are people. To you we are parents, set apart by our relationship to you. But also we are man and woman, conditioned by our own parents, by our past experiences, our religious understanding, our personal needs and shortcomings. We need love and security the same as you do. We want happiness. We crave companionship. Accept us, oh, do continue to accept us, as imperfect people trying to right past mistakes. Share our difficulties and disappointments; share our new hopes. Don't let's shut each other out." Children understand a considerable measure of that kind of explanation.

There is also a kind of parent who sees the questions coming before the break has been made and accepts maturity; accepts a quickened sense of his own limitations, a sharper look at his own ideals, a girding of the spiritual loins; a more sensitive awareness of the children's emotional tendrils trying to lay hold on something sturdy and

dependable which can bear their weight; an assurance of
the availability of guidance when it is sought in humility
and with true intent. To be sure, there are no cover-all
answers about what to do with an unhappy marriage but
a parent with determination to find an answer for himself
can often thereby obviate the more difficult questions of
his children.

Questions about the permanancy of his parents' marriage are really questions about his own marriage, especially to a young person approaching the marriage age.
To a direct question, "Will it last?" even a parent whose
own marriage is congenial has no completely assuring
answer. The only sure thing about the marriage relationship is that it will change, and the young fear change.
Of course "Will it last?" really means, "Will it succeed?
Will it maintain happiness?" And how shall a parent
say to a son or a daughter: "Success...happiness...
they are not the final measure of life. The measure of life
is *life*. Disaster may hold as much of life as success. Pain,
disappointment, regret — they too are the materials of life.
Immortality has been known to hide in dregs of hemlock.
So go right ahead. Your cup will be fuller and richer
this way."

Then he may wish to go on and point out the importance to a marriage of the partners being mature individuals. Marriage today has a certain advantage in the
fact that the exigencies of the times seem to have brought
about a state in which both members of the partnership,
the woman as well as the man, have a better chance for
personal development. Such growth may come through
the individual's developing his own ability to obviously
greater usefulness, or it may sometimes come through his
investing his creative energy in the other partner's development. But in either case it must be genuine growth in

order to yield the satisfaction which adult personality demands. Nowadays, economic conditions force both parents in an increasing proportion of marriages to become wage earners. Along with the disadvantages of such arrangement come distinct advantages in the form of varied contacts, the careful planning of time, new bases for companionship. In the rearing of children, also, the new economic necessity for two wage earners offers conditions which may be turned to advantage: the mother's heightened enjoyment of children whom she does not have on her hands twenty-four hours each day, the father's increased responsibility for the children, the children's greater opportunity for independence and initiative. The wife need not feel that she is crossing the accepted standards in going to work outside her home. Nor need the husband feel that he has failed in not supporting his wife adequately. For in creating the necessity for two wage earners, society has largely removed the odium. These psychological releases are of almost immeasurable value in promoting the respect and satisfaction necessary to contented marriage. When the ledger is drawn and the obvious disadvantages of the double-wage-earner setup are entered in bright red ink, there is still a long and comforting column of advantages to hearten the new marriage partners. And for the woman who is not a joint breadwinner, there is increasing opportunity for personal growth through social and civic service, through study groups, through club activities, through a dozen new devices of the modern inventive young matron. Every advantage may carry its particular hazard, but the advantage to modern marriage is nevertheless present.

But when a parent has totaled these and many other helps which modern society offers to modern marriage, he has still not said the most important thing which is that a young couple must still put much individual effort into achieving their own happiness. With so many hazards and uncertainties in the minds of the young it seems a world's wonder that so many get off to a good start. Parents must have more solid qualities than we sometimes give ourselves credit for, because our children do by-pass a heap of trouble, avoid a lot of pitfalls, and walk to the altar with a good firm step.

Hazards, for parents, on every side as well as behind and before. But sometimes they need only to be pointed out to be avoided. And sometimes we sail serenely over a jagged rock without even knowing it threatened our keel. Parenthood, grandparenthood, great-grandparenthood — when has a venturous voyage ever been free from risk of wave and swell, waterspout, hurricane, or too-too many barnacles.